FACTS

&

Figures

Basic Reading Practice

Third Edition

Patricia Ackert
with
Nicki Giroux de Navarro
and Jean Bernard

HH HEINLE & HEINLE PUBLISHERS
I(T)P AN INTERNATIONAL THOMSON PUBLISHING COMPANY
BOSTON, MASSACHUSETTS 02116 U.S.A.

• BOSTON • ALBANY • BONN • CINCINNATI • DETROIT • MADRID • MELBOURNE • MEXICO CITY •
• NEW YORK • PARIS • SAN FRANCISCO • SINGAPORE • TOKYO • TORONTO • WASHINGTON •

The publication of *Facts & Figures, Third Edition* was directed by the members of the ESL/EFL team at Heinle & Heinle:

Erik Gundersen, Senior Editor
Charlotte Sturdy, Market Development Director
Amy Mabley, Global Market Development Director
Maryellen Killeen, Production Services Coordinator
Stanley J. Galek, Vice President & Publisher
Amy Lawler, Managing Development Editor

Also participating in the publication of this program were:

Jill Kinkade, Assistant Editor
Marianne Bartow, Associate Market Development Director
Mary Beth Hennebury, Senior Manufacturing Coordinator
Thompson Steele Production Services Inc., Interior Designer and Page Production
Ko Design, Diana Coe, Cover Designer
Jonathan Stark, Image Resources Director
Evelyn Nelson, Director Global ESL Training & Development

CNN. is a registered trademark of Cable News Network.

Photograph Credits: Ian Cleghorn/Photo Researchers, p. 1; Michael Lajoie, p. 33; Superstock, p. 69; Mulvehill/The Image Works, p. 105; Skjold/The Image Works, p. 143; T. E. Eiler/Stock, Boston, p. 179; Joe Munroe/Photo Researchers, p. 219.

Library of Congress Cataloging-in-Publication Data

Ackert, Patricia.
    Facts & figures: basic reading practice / Patricia Ackert with Jean Bernard.—3rd ed.
        p.   cm.
Includes indexes.
ISBN 0-8384-0865-6
1. English language—Textbooks for foreign speakers. 2. Readers.
I. Bernard, Jean. II. Title. III. Title: Facts and figures.
PE1128. A2874 1999
428.6'4—dc21   98-43208
                                                                CIP

Manufactured in the United States of America
10   9   8   04

Contents

Unit 6 *Interesting People of the World*

Unit 7 *Exploration and Adventure*

Facts & Figures, Third Edition is a beginning reading skills text designed for students of English as a second or foreign language who have a basic vocabulary in English of about 300 words. This text teaches about 500 more words. It also teaches the reading skills of comprehension, finding the main idea, and using the context to understand vocabulary items. The CNN-based video clips provide students with a wealth of authentic language and the accompanying video activities give them the opportunity to go beyond the text by using the vocabulary they have learned in the unit while building their oral/aural fluency.

Facts & Figures is one in a series of reading skills texts. The complete series has been designed to meet the needs of students from the beginning to the high intermediate levels and includes the following:

- *Facts & Figures, Third Edition*..Beginning

- *Thoughts & Notions* ....High Beginning

- *Cause & Effect, Third Edition*..Intermediate

In addition to the student text, an instructor's manual, video cassette, and audio cassette are also available for *Facts & Figures.* The instructor's manual contains answers to all the exercises, a test for each unit, strategies for using news video in the classroom, and transcriptions of each video clip. The audio cassette contains recordings of each of the 35 readings in the text.

• Theme-based approach to reading. Each of the seven units has a theme such as animals, plants, explorations, or occupations. The beginning lessons have a text that is about a half page long. The length gradually increases to about a page. The texts in the first unit are purposely easy and cover information the students already know so that with this comparatively easy material, they can get used to the book, the class, and the instructor.

• Systematic presentation and recycling of vocabulary. One of the primary tasks of beginning students is developing a useful and personally relevant vocabulary base. In *Facts & Figures, Third Edition,* ten or twelve words are introduced in each lesson. These words appear in boldface type. Those underlined are illustrated or glossed in the margin. All of the new vocabulary items are used several times in the lesson, and then are systematically recycled throughout the text. All the words introduced in the text are listed in the "Vocabulary Index" located in the back of the book.

Because vocabulary is introduced gradually and then used repeatedly, it is best to teach the lessons in chronological order. Otherwise, students might be confronted with too many new vocabulary items in any given lesson.

• **Focus on grammatical structure.** The first two units use only the present tense, and the sentences are short. The past tense is introduced in Unit 3 and the present continuous in Unit 5. The only other tenses used are the past continuous and the future with *will* and *going to*. Subject, object, possessive, and reflexive pronouns are used. *Facts & Figures, Third Edition* also presents such connectors as and, but, so, then, because, or, and when. By using these, the text can include longer sentences that are still easy for the students to read.

Rationale for Various Exercise Types

• **Context Clues.** Starting with Unit 2, a context clue exercise at the beginning of each unit introduces some of the vocabulary for the following unit. This section is designed to pre-teach particularly important grammar.

• **Pre-reading Questions.** These questions provide a motivation for reading the text. Some of them are yes/no questions that can be answered by looking carefully at the illustration. They are designed simply to call to mind whatever knowledge of the subject the student may already have. Through close scrutiny of the illustration, the student begins to draw conclusions, putting logical reasoning into play. Some of the questions cannot be answered before the text is read. Students can look for the answers to these questions while reading the text. Some questions require student input and opinions.

• **Vocabulary.** The first exercise has sentences taken directly from the text. All new words are included. This is for practice in reading the sentences again and writing the new words.

• **Vocabulary (new context).** This exercise gives further practice with the new words in a different context but with the same meaning.

● **Vocabulary Review.** Vocabulary items are used in subsequent texts and exercises to give additional review. They are fill-ins or matching synonyms and antonyms.

● **Questions.** These comprehension questions are taken directly from the text. They can be done orally in class, and/or the students can write the answers as homework. Those marked with an asterisk are either inference or discussion questions.

● **Comprehension.** These are either true/false, true/false/no information, or multiple choice. There are also inference and discussion questions marked with an asterisk.

● **Main Idea.** Students must choose the main idea of the text from three possibilities.

● **Word Study.** A word study section is provided at the end of each unit. It reinforces structural points, such as verb forms, pronouns, and comparison of adjectives, that the students are learning in other classes. It also gives spelling rules for noun plurals and verb endings. Later units have charts of word forms. The exercises are not intended to be complete explanations and practice of the grammar points. The material in this section is included in the tests in the instructor's manual.

● **Writing.** Each unit closes with an optional writing exercise that the instructor may assign. The students may be asked to write answers to one, two, or all three of these questions.

● **Extension Activities.** Each unit ends with a four-page collection of high-interest, interactive tasks to help students practice the new vocabulary and the skills they have learned in more open-ended contexts.

New Features in the Third Edition

● **Audio Cassette.** Recordings of all the readings are provided on one tape. Listening to the readings is a tremendously helpful way for many students to comprehend new words and ideas.

- **Extension Activities.**
  - **CNN Video Activity**—The highlight of each set of Extension Activities is a short video-based lesson centered on a stimulating, authentic clip from the CNN video archives. Each video lesson follows the same sequence of activities:
    - *Before You Watch* encourages students to recall background knowledge based on their own experiences or from information presented in the readings.
    - *As You Watch* asks students to watch for general information such as the topic of the clip.
    - *After You Watch* gets students to expand on the main points of the video by establishing further connections to the reading passages, their own experiences, and their ideas and opinions.
  - **Activity Page**—Games found on this page encourage students to practice the vocabulary and structures found in that unit's lessons in a relaxed, open-ended way.
  - **Dictionary Page**—Exercises on this page offer students practice with dictionary skills based on entries from *The Basic Newbury House Dictionary.*

- **Skills Index.** This index provides teachers and students with a handy reference for all of the reading and writing skills introduced in *Facts & Figures,* as well as all of the grammatical structures found in the text.

Teaching Methods

After the class studies the introductory illustration and accompanying pre-reading questions, the teacher may choose to either read the text aloud, play it on tape, or ask students to read it silently. Then the class can do the exercises, with the instructor or students writing the answers on the board. For variety, the students might do the exercises together in small groups. Then the class as a whole can go over the exercises quickly.

Students need to understand the subject matter so they can answer the comprehension and main idea questions, but they should not be required to learn the information. It should be stressed to the students that the purpose of *Facts & Figures, Third Edition* is to teach reading skills and vocabulary, not information. Otherwise, they will be spending hours memorizing facts that they do not need to know.

The tests in the instructor's manual focus on reading skills by presenting students with a new text and set of questions related to the theme of the unit they have just studied.

Since students are not required to learn the information presented in the readings, they can go through the book fairly quickly. It is probably necessary to go through the first unit slowly, but after that, we suggest that the students do about one lesson together in class and one as homework each day. The students can do a lesson together in class. The instructor can then introduce the pre-reading questions and read the next text, assigning that lesson for homework. The next day, he or she can go over the assignment in class and introduce, read, and assign another. Students should read each text two or three times as homework. At the end of each lesson, they should test themselves on the boldface vocabulary items and memorize any that they have not learned through use.

Students should learn all of the material in the word study sections. It is all basic material that they need to know. The explanations are purposely very simple so that students can easily understand them. Most instructors will want to give further explanations as they present each part.

There is ample material for class discussions if the text is used in conjunction with a spoken English class. Alternatively, if students are enrolled in an intensive reading skills course, there is no need to discuss the content of the lessons, except to verify comprehension.

There are no timed readings. Students should be allowed to read at their own speed so that they have time to notice everything they possibly can about the English language.

Instructor's Manual

The student text for *Facts & Figures, Third Edition* is accompanied by a carefully developed instructor's manual. This teacher's component includes pedagogical notes, a section entitled "Using Authentic News Video in the ESL/EFL Classroom," transcriptions of the CNN video clips, an answer key for the student text, and tests for each of the seven units presented in *Facts & Figures*.

The tests include a vocabulary section like the first two exercises in the lessons. There is a short reading passage with comprehension and main idea questions. There are also questions on the material in the Word Study sections. Each test has 25 to 40 questions. The students should be able to do the tests in about 13 to 20 minutes, allowing a half minute for each item.

To the Student

We hope you enjoy reading this book.
You will learn a lot of English from it.
You can also learn a lot about the world.

Acknowledgments

The authors and publisher would like to thank the following individuals who offered helpful feedback and suggestions for the updated edition:

- Julia Cayuso—*University of Miami, (FL)*
- Martha Compton—*University of California, Irvine (CA)*
- Annette Fruehan—*Orange Coast College (CA)*
- Julia Karet—*Chaffey College (CA)*
- Mary O'Neill—*Northern Virginia Community College (VA)*
- Jorge Perez—*Southwestern College (CA)*
- Sara Storm—*California State University, Fullerton (CA)*
- Kent Sutherland—*Canada College (CA)*

Animals

The Kiwi

LESSON

LESSON

1

Pre-reading Questions

1. What is a kiwi?

2. Where does a kiwi live?

3. How many toes does it have?

1

The Kiwi

The **kiwi** lives **only** in New Zealand. It is a very **strange** bird because it cannot **fly.**

The kiwi is the same **size** as a chicken. It has no **wings** or **tail.** It does not have any
5 **feathers** like other birds. It has hair on its body. Each foot has four toes. Its **beak** (mouth) is very long.

A kiwi likes a lot of trees around it. It sleeps **during** the day because the sunlight
10 **hurts** its eyes. It can **smell** things with its nose. It is the only bird in the world that can smell things. The kiwi's eggs are very big.

There are only a few kiwis in New Zealand now. People never see them. The **government**
15 says that people cannot kill kiwis. New Zealanders want their kiwis to live.

There is a picture of a kiwi on New Zealand money. People from New Zealand are sometimes called kiwis.

beak · wing · tail

feather

■A■ Vocabulary

Put the right word in the blanks. The sentences are from the text.

government	smell	during	kiwi
kill	size	fly	only
wings	chicken	beak	tail
strange	hurts	feathers	body

1. It sleeps _____ the day because the sunlight
   _____ its eyes.
2. It is a very _____ bird because it cannot _____.
3. The _____ says that people cannot kill kiwis.
4. It can _____ things with its nose.
5. It has no _____ or _____.
6. The _____ lives _____ in New Zealand.
7. It does not have any _____ like other birds.
8. Its _____ (mouth) is very long.
9. The kiwi is the same _____ as a chicken.

■B■ Vocabulary (new context)

Put the right word in the blanks. These are new sentences for the same words.

during	pictures	kiwi	only
size	smells	wings	hair
hurts	strange	tail	feathers
tree	fly	beak	government

1. The _____ and a few other birds cannot fly.
2. A bluebird has blue _____.
3. Some students have a scholarship from their _____.
4. An airplane can _____ because it has
   _____.
5. What are you cooking? It _____ good.
6. My leg _____. I can't walk on it.
7. Most cats have a long _____.
8. A person has a mouth. A bird has a _____.
9. Some students are very _____. They want to learn
   English but they don't come to class.

10. I cannot buy this shirt. I have _____ three dollars.
11. What _____ shoes do you wear?
12. Most people work _____ the day and sleep at night.

C Questions

The asterisk (*) means you have to think of the answer. You cannot find it in the text.

1. Where does the kiwi live?
2. What is a kiwi?
3. How big is a kiwi?
4. Does a kiwi have feathers?
5. Does it have a tail and wings?
*6. How many toes does it have?
7. When does a kiwi sleep?
8. Can most birds smell?
9. Why can't people kill kiwis?
*10. Why does New Zealand have a picture of a kiwi on its money?

D Comprehension: True/False

Write *T* if the sentence is true. Write *F* if it is not true. The asterisk (*) means you have to think of the answer. You cannot find it in the text.

_____ 1. Kiwis live in Australia and New Zealand.
_____ 2. A kiwi has a tail but no wings.
_____ 3. A kiwi has a big beak.
_____ 4. It sleeps during the day because light hurts its eyes.
_____ *5. You can see a kiwi in some zoos in New Zealand.
_____ 6. The New Zealand government does not want all the kiwis to die.
_____ 7. A kiwi is like most other birds.

E Main Idea

Circle the number of the main idea of the text.

1. The kiwi is a strange New Zealand bird.
2. The kiwi sleeps during the day and has no tail or wings.
3. New Zealanders like kiwis.

The Camel

LESSON 2

Pre-reading Questions

1. Are all camels the same?

2. Where do camels live?

3. Do camels have long hair or short hair?

The Camel

The **camel** can go without water for a long time. Some people think it **stores** water in its **hump.** This is not true. It stores food in its hump. The camel's body changes the food into
5 fat. Then it stores the fat in its hump. It cannot store the fat **all over** its body. Fat all over an animal's body keeps the animal warm. Camels live in the **desert.** They do not want to be warm during the day.

10   The desert is very hot. The camel gets hotter and hotter during the day. It stores this **heat** in its body because the nights are **cool.**

    The Arabian camel has one hump. The Bactrian camel of Central Asia has two humps.
15 It **also** has long, **thick** hair because the winters are cold in Central Asia.

    There is a lot of sand in the desert. The camel has long **eyelashes.** Then the sand cannot go into the camel's eyes.
20   Arabic has **about** 150 words to **describe** a camel. Arabs need all these words because the camel is very important to them.

keeps

everywhere

noun for *hot*

a little cold

too

about = more or less/
  describe = to tell about

◼A◼ Vocabulary

Put the right word in the blanks. The sentences are from the text.

all over	during	eyelashes	hump
also	cool	thick	desert
stores	camel	describe	winters
sand	about	fat	heat

1. Arabic has _____ 150 words to _____ a camel.
2. The _____ can go without water for a long time.
3. The camel has long _____.
4. Some people think it _____ water in its _____.
5. Camels live in the _____.
6. It _____ has long, _____ hair because the winters are cold in Central Asia.
7. It cannot store the fat _____ its body.
8. It stores this _____ in its body because the nights are _____.

◼B◼ Vocabulary (new context)

Put the right word in the blanks. These are new sentences for the same words.

also	winters	about	hotter
camels	cool	heat	desert
during	food	all over	describe
hump	eyelashes	thick	store

1. We _____ milk, fruit, and vegetables in the refrigerator.
2. Fall is _____ in Canada. Winter is cold. Winter is _____ cold in Russia.
3. Can you _____ an elephant? What does it look like?
4. There are different animals _____ the world.
5. Some camels have one _____ and some have two.
6. Some people have long _____ by their eyes.
7. It does not rain very much in the _____.

8. Mark's engineering textbook is very ———————. It has more than 1,000 pages.
9. We cook food with ——————— from a stove.
10. Not many Arabs ride on ———————. Now they use cars.
11. Tom is ——————— 25 years old. Maybe he is 24 or 27.

C Questions

1. Where do camels live?
2. What does a camel store in its hump?
3. The camel doesn't store fat all over its body. Why?
4. Why does it store heat during the day?
5. Which camel has one hump? Which has two?
6. Why does a Bactrian camel have long, thick hair?
7. Why does a camel need long eyelashes?
8. Why does Arabic have 150 words to describe a camel?

D Comprehension

Put a circle around the letter of the best answer.

1. The camel can go without ——— for a long time.
   a. food
   b. water
   c. fat
   d. heat

2. It stores ——— in its hump.
   a. water
   b. heat
   c. food
   d. hair

3. The ——— camel has one hump.
   a. Arabian
   b. Bactrian

4. Long ——— keep sand out of the camel's eyes.
   a. thick hair
   b. humps
   c. eyelashes
   d. ears

5. The Bactrian camel has long, thick hair because ———.
   a. it lives in a hot desert
   b. it stores fat in its hump
   c. winters are cold in Central Asia
   d. the sand gets in its eyes

E Main Idea

Circle the number of the main idea of the text.

1. There are two kinds of camels.
2. The camel has a good body for life in the desert.
3. The camel stores food in its hump.

The Polar Bear

LESSON

3

Pre-reading Questions

1. What do polar bears eat?

2. Do polar bears like hot weather or cold weather?

3. Do polar bears live near trees?

The Polar Bear

The **polar bear** is a very big white bear. We call it the polar bear because it lives inside the Arctic Circle near the <u>North</u> Pole. There are no polar bears at the <u>South</u> Pole.

5 The polar bear lives in the **snow** and **ice.** At the North Pole there is only snow, ice, and water. There is not any land. You cannot see the polar bear in the snow because its coat is yellow-white. It has a very **warm** coat because
10 the weather is cold north of the Arctic Circle.

This bear is three meters long, and it **weighs** 450 kilos. It can stand up on its back legs because it has very **wide** feet. It can use its front legs like arms. The polar bear can **swim**
15 very well. It can swim 120 kilometers out into the water. It **catches** fish and sea animals for food. It goes into the sea when it is **afraid.**

People like to kill the polar bear for its beautiful white coat. The governments of
20 Canada, the United States, and Russia say that no one can kill polar bears now. They do not want all of these beautiful animals to die.

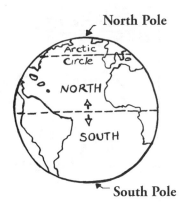

A Vocabulary

Put the right word in the sentences. The sentences are from the text.

polar	South	North	warm
kilos	catches	land	weighs
wide	sea	afraid	inside
bear	snow	swim	ice

1. The polar bear lives in the _____
    and _____.
2. The polar _____ is a very big white bear.
3. It goes into the sea when it is _____.
4. It has a very _____ coat because the weather is cold
    north of the Arctic Circle.
5. There are no polar bears at the _____ Pole.
6. The polar bear can _____ very well.
7. We call it the polar bear because it lives inside the Arctic Circle near the
    _____ Pole.
8. It _____ fish and sea animals for food.
9. This bear is three meters long, and it _____ 450 kilos.
10. It can stand up on its back legs because it has very _____
    feet.

B Vocabulary (new context)

Put the right word in the blanks. These are new sentences for the same
words.

swim	afraid	North	south
warm	weigh	ice	wide
snow	coat	bears	catch

1. There are brown and black _____ in North America.
2. How much do you _____? Fifty kilos?
3. Winter is cold. Spring is _____. Fall is cool.
4. Sometimes children are _____ of animals.
5. Do you like to _____ in a swimming pool?
6. Italy is _____ of France.

7. Do you want some ———————— in your Coke?
8. There is ———————— all over Canada in the winter.
9. The Sahara Desert is in ———————— Africa.
10. Tenth Street is a ———————— street. A log of cars can go on it at the same time.
11. Can you ———————— the ball?

C Vocabulary Review

Put *C* before the words about camels. Put *K* before the words about kiwis. Some of the words are not about camels or kiwis.

———————— 1. stores heat in its body
———————— 2. hump
———————— 3. tail
———————— 4. big eggs
———————— 4. goes without water
———————— 6. long, thick hair
———————— 7. eyelashes
———————— 8. beak
———————— 9. desert
———————— 10. wing
———————— 11. hair on its body
———————— 12. feather

D Questions

The asterisk (*) means you have to think of the answer.

1. Why do we call this bear the polar bear?
2. Why can't people see the polar bear very well?
3. Why does it have a warm coat?
4. How much does it weigh?
5. What does it eat?
6. Where does it go when it is afraid?
7. Why do people like to kill the polar bear?
8. What do the governments of Russia, the United States, and Canada say?
*9. Can a polar bear live near New Zealand?
*10. Why doesn't a polar bear eat fruit and vegetables?

E Comprehension

1. The polar bear lives _____.
   a. at the South Pole
   b. in warm countries
   c. near the North Pole
   d. on land

2. At the North Pole there is no _____.
   a. ice
   b. water
   c. snow
   d. land

3. You cannot see the polar bear in the snow because _____.
   a. it has a yellow-white coat
   b. it goes under the snow
   c. it can run very fast
   d. it goes into the water

4. The polar bear _____ for food.
   a. catches land animals
   b. looks for trees
   c. catches sea animals and fish
   d. looks for fruit and vegetables

5. When the polar bear is afraid, it _____.
   a. goes into the sea
   b. goes under the snow
   c. runs away
   d. stands up on its wide feet

6. The governments of Russia, Canada, and the United States say that _____.
   a. the polar bear is beautiful
   b. it has a warm coat
   c. no one can kill the polar bear
   d. it cannot live near the North Pole

F Main Idea

Circle the number of the main idea of the text.

1. People like to kill polar bears because they have beautiful warm, yellow-white coats.
2. Polar bears live north of the Arctic Circle in the snow and ice.
3. Polar bears live north of the Arctic Circle, eat fish and sea animals, and have warm, yellow-white coats.

The Hippopotamus

LESSON

4

Pre-reading Questions

1. Where does the hippopotamus live?
2. Does it like water?
3. Where is the baby hippo?

The Hippopotamus

The hippopotamus lives in the hot part of Africa. It is a **mammal.** That is, its babies are born **alive,** and they drink milk from the mother's body.

5 The hippopotamus is a **large** animal. It weighs four tons. Its **stomach** is seven meters long, but it eats only **plants.** It is a mammal, but it **spends** a lot of time in the water.

During the day it sleeps **beside** a river or a

10 **lake.** Sometimes it wakes up. Then it goes under the water to get some plants for food. It can close its nose and **stay** under water for ten minutes. Its ears, eyes, and nose are **high** up on its head. It can stay with its body under the

15 water and only its ears, eyes, and nose **above** the water. Then it can **breathe** the air.

At night the hippo walks on the land and looks for food. It never goes very far from the water.

20 A baby hippo often stands on its mother's back. The mother looks for food underwater. The baby rides on her back above the water.

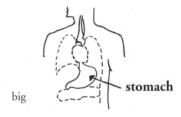

big   stomach

at the side of

over

lake

A Vocabulary

stomach	stay	beside	mammal
breathe	lake	plants	spends
above	alive	large	high

1. The hippopotamus is a _____ animal.
2. During the day it sleeps _____ a river or a
   _____.
3. It is a _____.
4. Its _____ is seven meters long, but it eats only
   _____.
5. It can close its nose and _____ under water for ten
   minutes.
6. It can stay with its body under the water and only its ears, eyes, and nose
   _____ the water.
7. Then it can _____ the air.
8. It is a mammal, but it _____ a lot of time in the water.
9. Its eyes, ears, and nose are _____ up on its head.

B Vocabulary (new context)

beside	lake	mammal	stomach
plants	stays	breathe	nose
large	above	spend	high

1. The camel is a _____, but the kiwi is a bird.
2. Food goes from your mouth into your _____.
3. How do you smell a beautiful flower? You _____ in with
   your nose.
4. Camels eat _____. Polar bears and kiwis eat meat.
5. I want to talk to you. Please sit _____ me.
6. Tom likes to _____ his free time in the Student Union.
   He _____ there a few hours every day.
7. Birds can fly _____ the trees.
8. _____ Geneva is a beautiful lake in Switzerland.
9. The polar bear is a _____ animal. It is very big.
10. New York has a lot of _____ buildings.

C Vocabulary Review

Put a circle around the letter of the best answer.

1. Can you _____ a polar bear? What does it look like?
   a. hurt   c. catch
   b. describe   d. store

2. Many birds fly _____ in the winter to a warmer place.
   a. north   c. south
   b. wing   d. wide

3. These birds fly _____ in the summer to a cooler place.
   a. north   c. south
   b. wing   d. wide

4. Roses _____ beautiful.
   a. swim   c. smell
   b. catch   d. hurt

5. The kiwi is a _____ bird.
   a. strange   c. hurt
   b. warm   d. wide

6. My hand _____. I can't write.
   a. flies   c. smells
   b. catches   d. hurts

D Questions

1. Where does the hippopotamus live?
*2. Is a kiwi a mammal?
3. How long is a hippo's stomach?
4. Does a hippo eat meat?
5. Why does a hippo go under water?
6. How can it stay under water for ten minutes?
*7. Can it breathe under water? Why?
8. What does it do at night?
9. Where does a baby hippo ride?
*10. Is a bear a mammal?

▐E▌ Comprehension: True/False/No Information

Put *T* if the sentence is true. Put *F* if it is false. Put *NI* if there is no information about the sentence.

_____ 1. Hippo babies are born alive.
_____ 2. Birds and hippos eat plants.
_____ 3. Hippos live under water.
_____ 4. A hippo can close its eyes.
_____ 5. A hippo breathes under water.
_____ 6. A hippo looks for food on the land during the day.
_____ 7. A hippo has long eyelashes to keep water out of its eyes.

▐F▌ Main Idea

1. The hippopotamus is a large African animal that spends a lot of time in the water and eats plants.
2. The hippopotamus has eyes, ears, and nose high up on its head.
3. The hippopotamus walks on the land at night, and it eats and sleeps during the day.

The Dolphin

LESSON

5

Pre-reading Questions

1. Are dolphins fish?

2. Where do dolphins live?

3. Do you see one dolphin or more than one?

The Dolphin

Can **dolphins** talk? Maybe they can't talk
with words, but they talk with **sounds.** They
show their feelings with sounds.

Dolphins **travel** in a **group.** We call a   three or more
5 group of fish a "school." They don't study, but
they travel **together.** Dolphins are mammals,
not fish, but they swim together in a school.

Dolphins talk to the other dolphins in the
school. They give information. They tell when
10 they are happy or sad or afraid. They say
"Welcome" when a dolphin comes back to the
school. They talk when they play.

They make a few sounds above water.
They make many more sounds under water.
15 People cannot hear these sounds because they
are very, very high. **Scientists** make tapes of the
sounds and study them.

Sometimes people catch a dolphin for a
large **aquarium.** (An aquarium is a zoo for fish.)
20 People can watch the dolphins in a show.
Dolphins don't like to be away from their school
in an aquarium. They are sad and **lonely.**

There are many stories about dolphins.
They help people. Sometimes they **save** some-
25 body's life. Dolphin meat is good, but people
don't like to kill them. They say that dolphins
bring good luck. Many people **believe** this.

A Vocabulary

together   mammals   travel   believe
dolphins   lonely   group   aquarium
save   show   sounds   scientists

1. Dolphins _____ in a _____.
2. Sometimes they _____ somebody's life.
3. Can _____ talk?
4. Sometimes people catch a dolphin for a large _____.
5. They are sad and _____.
6. They _____ their feelings with sounds.
7. _____ make tapes of their sounds and study them.
8. Many people _____ this.
9. They don't study, but they travel _____.
10. Maybe they can't talk with words, but they talk with

   _____.

B Vocabulary (new context)

lonely   dolphin   together   save
sounds   believe   scientists   aquarium
show   travel   feelings   group

1. The _____ is a mammal but it lives in the sea.
2. Many students at a large university feel _____. They
   don't have many friends.
3. Do you like to _____ to different countries?
4. Please _____ me your composition.
5. Children like to play _____ in the snow.
6. There is a _____ of Omani students in our class.
7. Is it true? Do you _____ it?
8. _____ study animals and many other things.
9. There are many interesting fish and sea animals at an _____.
10. You must _____ your money. Don't spend it on a new
    car.
11. It is difficult to pronounce some English _____.

C Vocabulary Review

Put these words under the right titles. Some words go under more than one title.

1. Parts of an Animal's Body   **2. Parts of a Person's Body**

eyelashes	hump	wing	feather
tail	beak	nose	arm
leg	stomach	hand	eyes

D Questions

1. Can dolphins talk?
2. What is a school of dolphins?
3. What do dolphins talk about?
4. When do they say "Welcome"?
5. Do they make more sounds above or under water?
6. Can people hear dolphin sounds? Why?
7. How does a dolphin feel in an aquarium?
*8. Do dolphins bring good luck?
*9. Dolphins are not fish. What is the difference between dolphins and fish?

E Comprehension

1. Dolphins talk with _____.
   a. words   c. sounds
   b. their hands   d. music

2. Dolphins talk when they _____.
   a. play   c. show
   b. listen   d. kill

3. They make more sounds _____.
   a. above water   c. for tapes
   b. under water   d. in school

4. Scientists study ———— of dolphins.
    a. shows
    b. schools
    c. aquariums
    d. tapes

5. Dolphins like to be ————.
    a. at an aquarium
    b. in their school
    c. lonely
    d. on a tape

6. What sentence is **not** true?
    a. A dolphin can save a person's life.
    b. People like to watch dolphins.
    c. Dolphins always bring good luck.
    d. A dolphin can talk with sounds.

F Main Idea

1. Dolphins use words to show how they feel and to give information.
2. Dolphins travel together and talk with sounds.
3. Dolphins live in the sea and in aquariums.
4. The dolphin is a mammal, and scientists can tape it.

Word Study

A Possessive Pronouns

These pronouns show that something belongs to somebody.

Example: **My** car is new.

Their hair is thick.

Singular	Plural
I – my	we – our
you – your	you – your
she – her	they – their
he – his	
it – its	

Put the right pronoun in the blanks.

1. The camel stores food in ————————— hump.
2. Maria likes ————————— classes this year.
3. I use ————————— dictionary every day.
4. Polar bears use ————————— front legs like arms.
5. Do you have ————————— cassette tapes with you?
6. Scientists listen to ————————— tapes.
7. Carlos and his family swim in ————————— pool every day.
8. David drives ————————— car to class.
9. We go to the university on ————————— bicycles.
10. A baby hippo rides on ————————— mother's back.

B Verbs—Present Tense

Put an **s** on the simple verb for the present tense. Do not put an **s** with **I, you, we,** or **they.**

a dolphin	play**s**	I	play
a girl	play**s**	you	play
a man	play**s**	we	play
she	play**s**	they	play
he	play**s**		
it	play**s**		

C Spelling

1. When a simple verb ends in **y** with a consonant before it, change the **y** to **i** and add **-es.**

     fly – flies   study – studies

2. When a simple verb ends in **y** with a vowel before it, add **-s.**

     play – plays   say – says

3. When a simple verb ends in **s, ch, sh, x,** or **z,** add **-es.**

     catch – catches   finish – finishes

4. Irregular:

     go – goes   do – does   have – has
     be – am, is, are

Change each sentence and make a new one. Use the word in parentheses. You must change some pronouns too.

    Example: (I)   They study every day.
                        I study every day.

(a polar bear)   1.   We catch fish and eat them.
(they)   2.   Mike usually flies home.
(I)   3.   Betty has a beautiful plant in her living room.
(people)   4.   David likes dolphin shows.
(we)   5.   They travel only in the summer.
(a dolphin)   6.   You play in the water.
(they)   7.   We go swimming in a lake in summer.
(Tom)   8.   I usually finish my work early.
(a mammal)   9.   People are born alive.
(Ann and Bill)   10.   Ali does his homework in the afternoon.

D Comparisons

Sometimes we compare two things. We tell how they are different. Add **-er** to short words (words with only one syllable) to compare two things. Use **than.**

> **Example:** A camel is big.
> A polar bear is **bigger than** a camel.
>
> Carlos is twenty years old. David is eighteen.
> Carlos is **older than** David.

Spelling: When a word has **one** syllable with **one** vowel in the middle and **one** consonant at the end, double the consonant and add **-er.** This is the one-one-one (1-1-1) rule.

> **Example:** big – bigger   hot – hotter

Put the right comparison form in the sentence.

(strange)   1.   A kiwi is _____ a bluebird.

(thick)   2.   A Bactrian camel's hair is _____ an Arabian camel's hair.

(hot)   3.   Oman is _____ Switzerland.

(warm)   4.   Italy is _____ France.

(large)   5.   Saudi Arabia is _____ Kuwait.

(tall)   6.   Marie is _____ Masako.

(fat)   7.   John is _____ Robert.

(young)   8.   My sister is _____ my brother.

(cold)   9.   Ice is _____ water.

(small)   10.   A dolphin is _____ a polar bear.

E Writing

Write real information in your answers.

1.   Which animal in *Unit I* is the most interesting to you? Why?
2.   Describe an important animal in your country.
3.   What can some animals do that people cannot do?

Video Highlights

A Before You Watch

1. What do you already know about dolphins? Write one fact.

   _____

2. What do you want to know about dolphins? Write a question.

   _____

3. Study the map. Then complete the sentences.

Honduras is between Guatemala and _____.

The north coast of Honduras is on the _____ Sea.

B As You Watch

What mammals are in the video?

_____ fish
_____ people
_____ camels
_____ polar bears
_____ dolphins

29

©CNN

1. Using the diagram below as an example, complete the exercise.
   Write facts that are *only* true for people in the left circle.
   Write facts that are *only* true for dolphins in the right circle.
   Write facts that are true for *both* dolphins and people in the middle.

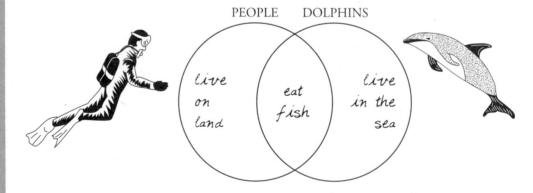

PEOPLE   DOLPHINS

live on land   *eat fish*   *live in the sea*

   a. live in the sea
   b. live on land
   c. can talk to each other
   d. are mammals

   e. have arms and legs
   f. eat fish
   g. swim together in schools
   h. make sounds under water

2. What is the most interesting fact you learned from the video? Write it here, then discuss it with your classmates.

   _____

   _____

Activity Page

A Crossword Puzzle

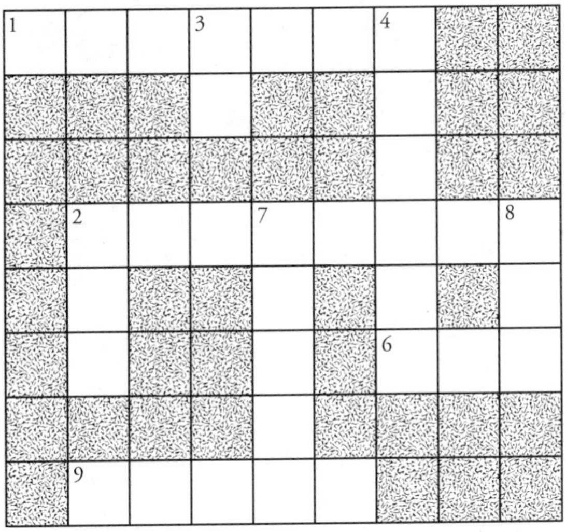

(crossword grid with numbered cells: 1, 3, 4 across top row; 2, 7, 8 in middle rows; 6 below; 9 at bottom)

Across

1. Camels, humans, and dolphins are all _____.
2. Both dolphins and humans show their _____ with sounds.
6. A large body of water
9. This land mammal lives in the desert and has a hump.

Down

2. This helps a dolphin to swim
3. Possessive form of "I"
4. Scientists study the _____ dolphins make under the water.
7. A hippopotamus is not small; it's _____.
8. Same as #6 across.

B Guess the Animal

Do this activity with a partner. You are A and your partner is B.

1. Think of an animal in Lessons 1–5. Do not tell your partner.
2. Ask your partner three questions. Each question must begin with "Does . . ." or "Is . . ."
   Example: Is it a mammal?
   Does it live on land?
   Is it white?
3. Answer your partner's questions with "Yes" or "No." Your partner can try to guess the name of the animal.

Dictionary Page

Finding Words in the Dictionary

1. *Guidewords* are at the top of every page in a dictionary. You can find them at the top left and right corners of the pages. For example, look up the word "desert" in your dictionary. What are the two guidewords at the top corners of the pages?

   _____ and _____

deprive   104   105   develop

deprive /dəˈpraɪv/ *verb* **deprived, depriving, deprives**
1 to take something away from: *Poverty deprived him of good food and medicine.*
2 to keep something from, (*synonym*) to deny: *Her illness deprived her of a chance to go to college.* –*adjective* **deprived** /dɪˈpraɪvd/; –*noun* **deprivation.**

depth /depθ/ *noun*
1 a distance below a surface: *The swimmer went down to a depth of five meters.*
2 a large amount: *I admire her depth of knowledge.*
3 a distance measured backwards from a line: *a building on a piece of land with a depth of 100 feet*

deputy /ˈdepyəti/ *noun, plural* **deputies** a person usually in a police function

desert (2) /dɪˈzɜrt/ *verb*
to leave forever: *People deserted the old town because the river flooded it.* –*noun* (act) **desertion,** (person) **deserter.**

deserve /dɪˈzɜrv/ *verb* **deserved, deserving, deserves**
to be worthy of, earn something good or bad: *A good worker deserves good pay.*

design /dɪˈzaɪn/ *noun*
1 the form or style in how something looks: *Their house was built in a modern design.*
2 a picture to show how something will be made: *Here is the design for our next magazine cover.*
3 the art of making designs: *She studies fashion design.*
4 a pattern that decorates: *I like the de...*

port... report... desc...ed the...
fire as it was happening.

description /dɪˈskrɪpʃən/ *noun*
an explanation: *His book gives a description of how to build a house.*

desert (1) /ˈdezərt/ *noun*
a dry place with little or no rain, making large areas of sand and rock with few plants or animals: *The Sahara Desert is in Africa.‖Southern California has a large desert.*   **desert**

w...s at her...every...y. Se...t on page 8a.

desktop computer or **desktop** /ˈdesktɑp/ *noun*
a computer small enough to fit on top of a desk: *We have three desktops in our office. See:* laptop.

despair /dɪˈspɛr/ *noun*
sadness without hope: *When she learned that she had cancer, she fell into despair.* –*verb* **to despair.**

desperate /ˈdespərɪt/ *adjective*
1 in immediate, very strong need: *Those poor people are desperate for food.*
2 wild and dangerous: *a desperate criminal willing to kill anyone to escape* –*adverb* **desperately;** –*noun* **desperation.**

despite /dɪˈspaɪt/ *preposition*
even though, in spite of: *Despite the fact that she is short, she is an excellent basketball player.*

dessert /dɪˈzɜrt/ *noun*
the last course in a meal, usually a sweet dish, such as cake, fruit, etc.: *We had apple pie and coffee for dessert.*

destination /ˌdestəˈneɪʃən/ *noun*
the place where someone is going or something is being sent: *The destination of our trip is San Francisco.*

destiny /ˈdestəni/ *noun, plural* **destinies**
1 the influence of uncontrollable forces on your life: *It was destiny, not an accident, that brought the two friends together.*

...fur...fin...The...ow of

to...move...separa...di...nect: *We need a carpenter to detach this bookshelf from the wall.* –*adjective* **detachable;** –*noun* (act) **detachment.**

detail /ˈditeɪl/ *noun*
1 a small matter, usually of little importance: *There is one detail in the plan that is unclear to me.*
2 small, fine parts: *This painting is rich with detail.* –*verb* **to detail.**

detect /dɪˈtɛkt/ *verb*
to uncover, find: *They detected a problem in the computer and fixed it.* –*noun* (act) **detection.**

detective /dɪˈtɛktɪv/ *noun*
a police officer (or private investigator)

whose work is getting information about crimes: *a police detective*

detector /dɪˈtɛktər/ *noun*
a device used to locate the presence of something: *Metal detectors are used in airports to find guns.*

detergent /dɪˈtɜrdʒənt/ *noun*
a strong soap that removes dirt and stains caused by grease, tea, blood, etc.: *This laundry detergent can remove grass stains from clothes.*

deteriorate /dɪˈtɪriəˌreɪt/ *verb* **deteriorated, deteriorating, deteriorates**
to fall into bad condition, become weak: *The old man's health has deteriorated.* –*noun* **deterioration.**

...se...road...ed wh...e th...is closed for repair: *Signs directed traffic to a detour.* –*verb* **to detour.**

devastate /ˈdevəˌsteɪt/ *verb* **devastated, devastating, devastates**
to destroy completely: *A storm devastated the island.* –*noun* **devastation.**

develop /dəˈvɛləp/ *verb*
1 to happen, occur: *Before making any plans to travel, let's see what develops when the storm arrives.*
2 to change a place by building: *They're going to develop this open land into a shopping center.*
3 to process: *to develop photographic film*

2. Camels live in the *desert*. Think of three more places where animals live. Write these places in alphabetical order in the left column.

Places where animals live	Page number	Guidewords	
a. *desert*	*104*	*deprive*	*develop*
b. _____	_____	_____	_____
c. _____	_____	_____	_____
d. _____	_____	_____	_____

3. Look up the words in your dictionary. For each word, write the page number and the guidewords at the top of the pages.

How? Why?

Context Clues

Sometimes you can understand a new word from the other words in the sentence. Read each sentence. Then choose the meaning of the new word. *Do not use your dictionary.* These are new words for this unit.

1. A cat can **climb** a tree. A camel cannot.
   a. sit under
   b. go up
   c. walk near
   d. fly into

2. Fish live in lakes, rivers, and **oceans.**
   a. seas
   b. north
   c. trees
   d. south

3. Queen Elizabeth II is a very **famous** woman.
   a. everyone likes her
   b. everyone studies about her in English class
   c. everyone knows about her
   d. everyone talks to her

4. It is easy to make a salad. **Mix** some lettuce, tomatoes, and cucumber.
   a. put together
   b. eat
   c. take out of the refrigerator
   d. buy

5. Indonesia, the Philippines, Senegal, and Cuba are in the **tropics.**
   a. hot, dry countries
   b. cold, dry countries
   c. cold, wet countries
   d. hot, wet countries

6. Paul **enjoys** sports. He plays soccer and basketball. He watches sports on television.
   a. looks at
   b. likes
   c. plays
   d. watches

7. A ping pong ball is **small.** A basketball is large.
   a. old
   b. little
   c. new
   d. big

8. A polar bear runs **toward** the sea when it is afraid.
   a. from
   b. in
   c. to
   d. of

9. Mrs. Mora **feeds** her birds every day.
   a. washes
   b. breathes
   c. saves
   d. gives food to

10. **Both** Isamu and Kumiko are from Japan.
    a. the two of them
    b. not any
    c. the five of them
    d. all of them

11. This is a **difficult** problem: $7,958,395 \div 9687$.
    a. not easy
    b. thick
    c. easy
    d. cool

12. Mr. Baker is 75 years old **so** he can't play baseball.
    a. He likes to play baseball.
    b. He doesn't want to play baseball.
    c. He plays baseball every day.
    d. He can't play baseball because he is 75 years old.

13. Mr. Baker is 75. He can't hear sounds very well. He is **hearing impaired.**
    a. can't see well
    b. can't walk well
    c. can't hear well
    d. can't run well

14. Tom wants a **whole** sandwich. I want only half of a sandwich.
    a. all of it
    b. part of it
    c. some of it
    d. 1/4 of it

Why Are Elevators Important?

LESSON

1

Pre-reading Questions

1. Why do we have elevators?

2. Do all buildings have elevators?

3. Do you use elevators? Where?

Why Are Elevators Important?

An **elevator** is **wonderful.** It is **really** only a small room. Rooms usually stay in one place. Elevators travel up and down all day long.

Sometimes a worker stands in the elevator.
5 He or she runs it up and down. In **modern** elevators there is no worker. The people walk in. They know what floor they want. They push a **button** and the elevator goes to that floor. It is all very fast and easy.

10 Elevators are very important to us. Why? Think about a tall building. Maybe it has twenty floors. Maybe it has fifty or more. Who can walk up all those **stairs?** Maybe people can **climb** them one time. Can someone climb thirty floors
15 to an office every day? Can small children walk up to their apartment on the twenty-fourth floor? Can their mother and father **carry** food up all those stairs? Of course not.

We can have high buildings because we
20 have elevators. We **could** not have all the beautiful tall buildings in the world without elevators. They are really wonderful.

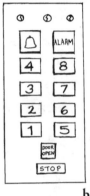

buttons

climb stairs

A   Vocabulary

worker	stairs	apartment	elevator
button	wonderful	modern	carry
really	climb	office	could

1. Who can walk up all those _____?
2. An _____ is _____.
3. Can their mother and father _____ food up all those stairs?
4. It is _____ only a small room.
5. Maybe people can _____ them one time.
6. They push a _____ and the elevator goes to that floor.
7. In _____ elevators there is no worker.
8. We _____ not have all the beautiful tall buildings in the world without elevators.

B   Vocabulary (new context)

stairs	modern	could	elevator
really	floor	worker	climb
buttons	wonderful	carry	push

1. Tokyo has a lot of high buildings. It is a _____ city.
2. You usually breathe hard when you walk up a lot of _____.
3. A group of people can ride together in an _____.
4. A bus can _____ a lot of people at one time.
5. Dolphins cannot _____ talk. They use sounds, not words.
6. Modern telephones have the numbers on _____.
7. Cats like to _____ trees.
8. Children think that a zoo is a _____ place to visit.
9. _____ you please help me for a minute?

C Vocabulary Review

breathe	describe	beside	sound
group	together	believe	save
scientists	show	aquarium	lonely
during	store	all over	cooler

1. Can you _____ an aquarium? Tell me about one.
2. Some _____ teach at universities and some work in laboratories.
3. There are two small tables _____ the sofa.
4. There are beautiful plants _____ the park.
5. Don't walk to class every day. Buy a bicycle. You can _____ time.
6. I don't _____ you. It isn't true.
7. Keiko is _____. She wants to see her friends and family.
8. Maria and Tony usually study _____.
9. An _____ is an interesting place to visit.
10. It is _____ under a tree than in the sun.

D Questions

1. What is an elevator, really?
2. How is an elevator different from other rooms?
3. Does a worker run a modern elevator?
4. How do people make an elevator go up and down?
5. Can people walk up twenty or forty floors every day?
6. Why can we have high buildings?

E Comprehension

1. An elevator is a small _____.
   a. room
   b. building
   c. stairs
   d. button

2. In modern elevators there is no _____.
   a. button
   b. light
   c. worker
   d. travel

3. An elevator travels _____.
   a. inside and outside   c. under and above
   b. in and out   d. up and down

4. People _____ climb thirty floors every day.
   a. like to   c. can
   b. cannot   d. want to

5. We can have _____ because we have elevators.
   a. high buildings   c. old buses
   b. new cars   d. wide streets

F Main Idea

1. People cannot climb a lot of floors in a tall building.
2. We can have high buildings because we have elevators.
3. An elevator is a small room.

Why Is the Sea Salty?

LESSON

Pre-reading Questions

1. Is a sea the same as a lake?

2. How is a lake different from a sea?

3. Is there land in the picture?

Why Is the Sea Salty?

There is a lot of **salt** on the <u>earth,</u> and it **mixes** very well with water.

There is some salt in all water. Water on the land runs into lakes and rivers. The water
5   from most lakes goes into rivers. These rivers run into the seas and <u>**oceans.**</u> They carry a little salt with them. Some of the ocean water **moves** into the air and <u>**clouds.**</u> It **evaporates.** Salt cannot evaporate. It stays in the ocean.
10   The water in the oceans has more salt than river water. Ocean water is about 3 1/2% (three and a half **percent**) salt. Some seas have more salt than others.

Some lakes do not have a river to carry the
15   water and salt away. Some of the water <u>**leaves**</u> the lakes. It evaporates, but the salt cannot. These lakes are very salty. There are two **famous** lakes like this. They are the Dead Sea in the Middle East and the Great Salt Lake in
20   the state of Utah in the United States. They are much saltier than the Atlantic Ocean and the Pacific Ocean.

world

seas

goes away from

clouds

A Vocabulary

evaporates	salt	leaves	percent
stays	moves	clouds	land
oceans	earth	mixes	famous

1. Ocean water is about three and a half _____ salt.
2. There is a lot of _____ on the _____, and it _____ very well with water.
3. Some of the water _____ the lakes.
4. There are two _____ lakes like this.
5. These rivers run into the seas and _____.
6. Some of the ocean water _____ into the air and _____.
7. It _____.

B Vocabulary (new context)

evaporates	earth	percent	famous
salt	state	earth	ocean
clouds	others	water	mix
moves	river	leave	student

1. Two of the students have to _____ the class early.
2. The _____ is round. It _____ around the sun.
3. Many people put _____ on their food.
4. Muhammad Ali was a _____ boxer.
5. Some people put sugar in their coffee. Then they _____ it with a spoon.
6. Some of the water in a swimming pool _____.
7. The Pacific _____ is bigger than the Atlantic Ocean.
8. There are beautiful white _____ in the sky today.
9. Eighty _____ of the class are men.

C Vocabulary Review

Underline the word that does not belong with the other two.

Example: red, <u>book,</u> blue

1. zoo, aquarium, university
2. lake, snow, ice
3. elevator, stairs, car
4. together, modern, new
5. polar bear, dolphin, kiwi
6. carry, climb, walk up
7. cool, warm, thick
8. scientist, teacher, saltier

D Questions

1. What does salt mix well with?
2. Is there salt in lakes and rivers?
3. Where does river water go?
4. Where does some of the ocean water go?
5. Where does the salt in the ocean go?
6. Which has more salt, rivers or oceans?
7. Why are some lakes very salty?
8. Name two famous salty lakes.
9. What is Utah? Where is it?
10. Which is saltier, the Atlantic Ocean or the Dead Sea?
*11. Are there fish in the Dead Sea?

E Comprehension: True/False

_____ 1. Salt mixes with water.
_____ *2. Clouds have salt in them.
_____ 3. Water on the land moves into lakes and rivers.
_____ 4. There is salt in rivers.
_____ 5. Rivers have more salt than oceans.
_____ 6. Salt evaporates.

_____ 7. Ocean water is about 2 1/4% salt.
_____ *8. Water leaves some lakes only in rivers.
_____ · 9. Great Salt Lake is in the United States.

F Main Idea

1. The sea is salty because water evaporates and salt doesn't.
2. The sea is salty because rivers run into oceans.
3. Water moves from the land to rivers to oceans to clouds and to the land again.

How Can a Plant Kill?

LESSON

Pre-reading Questions

1. Is everything in the picture alive? What is not alive? Why?

2. Did you ever get sick from eating a plant?

3. Can a plant run away?

How Can a Plant Kill?

People **kill.** Animals kill. Animals and people kill for food, or they kill their **enemies.** People and animals can move around and find something to kill. They can run away from an

5   enemy. They can kill it **if** it is necessary.

enemies ≠ friends

Many **kinds** of animals eat plants. The plants cannot run away from their enemies. Some plants make **poison.** If an animal eats part of the plant, it gets sick or dies. Animals

10 learn to stay away from these plants. There are many kinds of plants that make poison. Most of them **grow** in the desert or in the **tropics.**

hot, wet countries

Today **farmers** use many kinds of poison on their **farms.** Most of these poisons come

15 from petroleum, but petroleum is **expensive.** Scientists **collect** poisonous plants and study them. Maybe farmers can use **cheap** poison from plants **instead of** expensive poison from petroleum.

costs a lot

cheap ≠ expensive

A Vocabulary

kill	tropics	farmers	instead of
enemies	scientists	poison	cheap
plant	if	grow	farms
kinds	run away	collect	expensive

1. Many _____ of animals eat plants.
2. Animals and people kill for food, or they kill their _____.
3. Today _____ use many kinds of poison on their

   _____.
4. Scientists _____ poisonous plants and study them.
5. Some plants make _____.
6. Maybe farmers can use _____ poison from plants

   _____ expensive poison from petroleum.
7. Most of them _____ in the desert or in the

   _____.
8. They can kill it _____ it is necessary.
9. Most of these poisons come from petroleum, but petroleum is

   _____.
10. People _____.

B Vocabulary (new context)

expensive	tropics	petroleum	grow
cheap	scientist	collect	if
instead of	farm	kind	kill
most	farmers	poison	enemies

1. David's family has a big _____. They are

   _____.
2. A Mercedes Benz is an _____ car.
3. Please come to the Student Union at 12:00 _____ you
   can.
4. Malaysia, Togo, and Nigeria are in the _____.
5. Please write the answers on paper _____ in the book.
6. Ali, please _____ all the students' papers.
7. Some things we use in the garden are _____. We must
   keep them away from children.

8. People are the only _____ of polar bears.
9. What _____ of car do you have?
10. _____ clothes are not usually very good.
11. Children _____ very fast. They need new clothes every few months.

C Vocabulary Review

Find a word or words in Column B that mean the same as a word in Column A. Write the letter and word from Column B beside the word from Column A. The first one is done for you.

Column A
1. earth <u>d. world</u>
2. ocean _____
3. large _____
4. climb _____
5. percent _____
6. together _____
7. warm _____
8. cool _____
9. leave _____
10. modern _____
11. breathe _____

Column B
a. go
b. %
c. new
d. world
e. go up
f. take air into the body
g. a little hot
h. sea
i. button
j. big
k. lonely
l. a little cold
m. in a group

D Questions

1. Why do people and animals kill?
2. Can plants run away from an enemy?
3. What do some plants make?
4. What happens to an animal that eats this poison?
5. What do animals learn about these plants?
6. Where do most poisonous plants grow?
*7. Why do farmers use poison on their farms?

8. Where do most poisons come from?
9. Why do scientists collect and study poisonous plants?

E Comprehension

1. Animals and people kill their _____.
   a. poisons   c. plants
   b. enemies   d. farmers

2. _____ cannot move around.
   a. Plants   c. Farmers
   b. Animals   d. Scientists

3. An animal _____ if it eats a poisonous plant.
   a. gets sick or dies   c. moves around
   b. runs away   d. studies the poison

4. Most poisonous plants grow in the desert or in the _____.
   a. farms   c. Arctic Circle
   b. tropics   d. laboratories

5. _____ use many kinds of poisons.
   a. Scientists   c. Farmers
   b. Workers   d. Animals

6. Most of these poisons come from _____.
   a. plants   c. petroleum
   b. deserts   d. the tropics

7. Scientists _____ poisonous plants.
   a. use   c. buy
   b. run away from   d. collect

8. Poison from plants is _____ than poison from petroleum.
   a. cheaper   c. more expensive
   b. more afraid   d. cooler

F Main Idea

1. Some plants make poisons, and maybe farmers can use them.
2. Plants make poison because they cannot run away from their enemies.
3. Scientists study poisonous plants because farmers want to use them.

How Can We Have
Farms in the Sea?

Pre-reading Questions

1. What are the people doing with the fish?

2. How do the people carry the fish?

3. Are the fish big or little?

How Can We Have Farms in the Sea?

Farmers grow plants and animals on their farms. Is it also **possible** to have a farm in the sea?

People in many countries grow <u>**freshwater**</u>   not salty
5 fish from eggs. They move the small fish into lakes and rivers. The fish live and grow there. People go fishing in these lakes and rivers. They <u>**enjoy**</u> catching fish. Fish is also good food.   like

Now Japan grows saltwater fish. Most of
10 them are yellowtail fish. Workers grow the fish from eggs. Every time they <u>**feed**</u> the fish, they   give food to play tapes of **piano music.** The fish learn that piano music means food.

When the fish are <u>**small,**</u> the Japanese put   little
15 them in the ocean near the land. The fish find some of their **own** food. Workers also feed them. They play the same piano music. The fish **already** know this music. They swim <u>**toward**</u> it and find the food. In a few months   to
20 the fish are large. The Japanese play the same music. The fish swim toward it and the workers catch them.

The Japanese get about 15 percent of their seafood from farms in the ocean.

piano

A Vocabulary

music	piano	freshwater	possible
seafood	small	toward	lakes
already	own	feed	enjoy

1. When the fish are _____, the Japanese put them in the ocean near the land.
2. Is it also _____ to have a farm in the sea?
3. The fish _____ know this music.
4. They swim _____ it.
5. People in many countries grow _____ fish from eggs.
6. They _____ catching fish.
7. Every time they _____ the fish, they play tapes of _____ _____.
8. The fish find some of their _____ food.

B Vocabulary (new context)

feed	small	possible	toward
near	freshwater	music	own
enjoy	swim	already	piano

1. The Honda is a _____ car.
2. Do you like _____ fish or saltwater fish?
3. You _____ know a lot of English words.
4. Rivers run _____ the sea.
5. Is it _____ to travel to the moon?
6. Do you _____ snow and cold weather?
7. Can you play the _____?
8. Do you enjoy listening to _____?
9. Babies cannot cook their own food. We have to _____ them.
10. Do you ride to class with a friend or do you have your _____ car?

C   Vocabulary Review

Match each word in Column A with its opposite word in Column B. Write the letter and word from Column B next to the word in Column A. The first answer is done for you.

Column A

1. cool ___d. warm___
2. black _____
3. north _____
4. cannot _____
5. travel _____
6. false _____
7. old _____
8. leave _____
9. spend _____
10. under _____

Column B

a. white
b. true
c. modern
d. warm
e. stay home
f. cloud
g. save
h. mix
i. south
j. stay
k. can
l. above

D   Questions

1. Is it possible to have a farm in the ocean?
2. Why do people grow freshwater fish?
3. What country grows saltwater fish?
4. What do the Japanese do when they feed the fish?
5. What do the fish learn?
6. When do the workers put the fish in the ocean?
7. When do the workers play the same piano music?
8. Why do the fish swim toward this music?
9. Why do the workers play music when the fish are large?
10. How much food does Japan get from fish farms in the ocean?
*11. Do these fish like piano music? Why?
*12. Why are fish farms important to the world?

E   Comprehension: True/False

_____ 1. People can grow freshwater and saltwater fish.
_____ 2. The Japanese move the fish into the sea when they are large.
_____ 3. Piano music means food to most people.
_____ *4. Fish and birds grow from eggs.
_____ 5. All fish think that piano music means food.
_____ 6. The Japanese use piano music to catch fish.
_____ 7. Fish on ocean farms find some of their own food.
_____ 8. The Japanese grow about five percent of their saltwater fish on farms.

F   Main Idea

1. The Japanese use piano music on their saltwater farms.
2. It is possible to grow freshwater fish and saltwater fish on farms.
3. The Japanese get about 15 percent of their seafood from farms.

How Do Hearing-Impaired People Talk?

LESSON

5

Pre-reading Questions

1. What are the hands doing?

2. What is the woman doing?

3. Why do some people talk with their hands?

How Do Hearing-Impaired People Talk?

Hearing-impaired people cannot hear sounds well. How do they "hear" words and talk?

Many hearing-impaired people use American **Sign** Language (ASL). They talk with their hands.
5   Sometimes two hearing-impaired people talk to **each other.** They **both** use ASL. Sometimes a person who can hear **interprets** for hearing-impaired people. The person listens to someone talking, and then he or she makes hand signs.
10   There are two kinds of sign language. One kind has a sign for every letter in the alphabet. The person spells words. This is finger spelling. The other kind has a sign for **whole** words. There are about five thousand (5,000) of these signs.
15   They are signs for verbs, things, and **ideas.**

Some of the signs are very easy, for example, *eat, milk,* and *house.* You can see what they mean. Others are more **difficult,** for example, *star, egg,* or *week.*
20   People from any country can learn ASL. They don't speak words. They use signs, **so** they can understand people from other countries.

ASL is almost like a **dance.** The whole body talks. American Sign Language is a beau-
25   tiful language.

two of them

star

all of it

dance

A Vocabulary

ideas	hearing-impaired	difficult	star
each other	example	interprets	both
so	whole	sign	dance

1. Others are more _____, for example,
    _____, *egg*, or *week*.
2. Sometimes two hearing-impaired people talk to _____.
3. They _____ use ASL.
4. _____ people cannot hear sounds well.
5. ASL is almost like a _____.
6. The other kind has a sign for _____ words.
7. Sometimes a person who can hear well _____ for
    hearing-impaired people.
8. They use signs, not words, _____ they can understand
    people from other countries.
9. Many hearing-impaired people use American _____
    Language.
10. They are signs for verbs, things, and _____.

B Vocabulary (new context)

difficult	so	finger	dance
hearing-impaired	each other	idea	stars
sign	interprets	both	whole

1. The class wants to have a party. This is a good _____.
2. Mary cannot hear well. She is _____.
3. Ali works for the government. He _____ Arabic and
    English.
4. A large _____ says "No Smoking."
5. Masako and Carlos speak English to _____.
6. Nadia and David _____ study engineering.
7. You cannot see the _____ in the sky during the daytime.
8. Japanese is a _____ language. English is easy.
9. It is late _____ we cannot study any more.
10. The _____ class is here today. Everyone is here.
11. There is a _____ for foreign students on Saturday.

C Vocabulary Review

evaporates	famous	clouds	enemies
kind	expensive	if	cheaper
poison	collect	tropics	instead of
possible	music	already	enjoy

1. There are a lot of _____ in the sky today. It is cloudy.
2. Michael Jackson is a _____ singer.
3. The weather is hot and wet in the _____.
4. Do you _____ movies?
5. What _____ of bicycle do you have?
6. Please tell me _____ I talk too fast.
7. Water _____ into the air.
8. It is 8:58 and the students are _____ in their seats for their nine o'clock class.
9. Are apartments _____ or cheap in your city?
10. A bicycle is _____ than a car.
11. Some students listen to _____ when they study.

D Questions

1. How do many hearing-impaired people "talk"?
2. How does a person interpret for hearing-impaired people?
*3. How many signs are there for finger spelling?
4. How many word signs are there?
5. Why are some signs easy?
6. Why can people from different countries talk to each other with ASL?
7. Why is ASL almost like a dance?
*8. Why is ASL a beautiful language?

E Comprehension: True/False/No Information

_____ 1. Hearing-impaired people cannot hear sounds well.
_____ 2. A person who interprets for hearing-impaired people cannot hear.
_____ 3. There are more signs for words than for letters.
_____ 4. Japanese people use ASL.

_____ 5. Finger spelling has signs for numbers.
_____ 6. Africans cannot learn ASL because they don't speak English.
_____ 7. Only the hands move in ASL.
_____ 8. It is difficult for children to learn ASL.

F   Main Idea

1. ASL helps hearing-impaired people talk, but it is difficult to learn.
2. There are two kinds of sign language.
3. ASL is a beautiful language that helps hearing-impaired people talk to others.

Word Study

A Questions: Present Tense

be: Put **be** before the subject.

	subject	verb	
Example:	**Fish**	**are**	animals.
Are	**fish**		animals?

other verbs: Put **do/does** at the beginning of the sentence. Use the simple verb.

	subject	verb	
Example:	**Workers**	**move**	the fish into the sea.
Do	**workers**	**move**	the fish into the sea?

	subject	verb	
A	**worker**	**moves**	the fish.
Does	**a worker**	**move**	the fish?

Change each sentence to a question.

1. A large house is expensive.
2. Bill does his homework in the afternoon.
3. Rivers run toward the ocean.
4. Many people drink coffee.
5. Mary is a good tennis player.
6. Helen feeds her cat every morning.
7. Tony has his own car.
8. An elevator goes up and down.
9. Kiwis are strange birds.
10. I am late.

B There is/there are

Use **there is** before a singular noun. Then use **it**.

Example: **There is an elevator** in our apartment building. **It** is near the stairs.

Use **there are** before a plural noun. Then use **they.**

Example: **There are farms** in the sea. **They** are in Japan.

Look at the noun after the blank. Then write *there is* or *there are* in the first blank. Write *it* or *they* in the second blank.

1. _____ a kiwi in our zoo. _____ sleeps during the day.
2. _____ two black bears also. _____ come from Canada.
3. _____ a chair beside the window. _____ is blue.
4. _____ wonderful mountains in India. _____ are in the north.
5. _____ buttons in the elevator. _____ have lights inside them.
6. _____ a famous park in New York. _____ has a lot of big trees.
7. _____ some beautiful birds in the zoo. _____ come from the tropics.
8. _____ a small piano in the hall. _____ is for the student program tonight.

C -er = a person

Example: Mr. Brown is a **teacher.** He **teaches** English.

Add *-er* to each word. Then put the new words in the blanks. Use the plural if it is necessary.

play	work	farm	box
interpret	speak	listen	sing

1. Keiko is an _____. She speaks both Japanese and English.
2. Mr. and Mrs. Clark are _____. They have a large cotton farm.
3. Sarah Green is a wonderful _____. She sings in Europe and North America.
4. In the morning class, five students speak Arabic. In the afternoon class, there are seven Arabic _____.

5. Bill is not a good _____. He talks all the time and doesn't listen.
6. Abdullah is a very good soccer _____.

D Compound Words

A compound word is two words together. They make one word. The meaning is like the meaning of the two words.

Example: **sun + light = sunlight** (light from the sun)

Put the right words in the blanks.

summertime	seafood	daytime	yellowtail
sunlight	underline	stoplight	bedroom

1. Gina likes fish and other _____. She doesn't eat very much meat.
2. Read each sentence. Put a circle around the subject. _____ the verb.
3. Most people work during the _____. A few people work at night.
4. Be careful when you drive. If the _____ is red, you must stop.
5. People eat in the dining room. They sleep in the _____.

E Writing

Write real information in your answers.

1. Which lesson in *Unit 2* is the most interesting to you? Why?
2. What information in *Unit 2* is new for you?
3. Think of something you know about. Write a "how" or a "why" question about it. Then answer the question.

Video Highlights

Q: How old is she?

A: I think she's about 60.

1. Look at the woman in this picture.
   What do you want to know about her?
   Write three questions.
   Practice asking and answering
   your questions with a partner.

2. The video you are going to watch
   is about a new idea. The name of
   this idea is "ecotourism." This word
   has two parts:

> *eco*—the natural world
> *tourism*—traveling for pleasure

What do you think "ecotourism" means? The picture below shows one
example. Discuss your idea with your classmates.

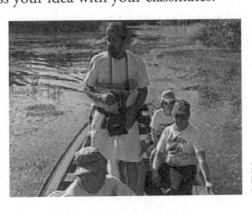

©CNN

65

B As You Watch

Which of these sentences about Silveria de Souza are true?

_____ She has eight children.

_____ She is a tour guide.

_____ She sells things to tourists.

_____ She is a farmer.

C After You Watch

1. Read about the rain forest in Brazil.

About ten million people live in the warm Amazon rain forest. Many of them clear parts of the forest for farms. This is called deforestation. The Brazilian farmers cut the forest down so they can grow crops and feed their families. Ten percent of the famous Amazon rain forest is gone now.

Ecotourism is a modern idea that tries to protect the rain forest. Tourists travel from all

over the world. They come to enjoy the forest and learn about nature. A tour guide leads a group through the great tropical forest. They stay at hotels in the villages and buy local handicrafts. Ecotourism brings jobs and money to the people who live in the Amazon. They do not have to destroy the rain forest just to make a living.

2. Write two questions about the rain forest in Brazil. Begin your questions with "Why" and "How." Discuss your questions with your classmates.

1. Why _____ ?

2. How _____ ?

Activity Page

A Word Search

Find and circle the words in the search list that are hidden in the grid below. There are fourteen vocabulary words in all.

H	R	T	C	L	I	M	B	A	P	T	W	Z	V
M	L	K	D	B	Y	O	P	Q	N	G	M	I	J
E	V	A	P	O	R	A	T	E	V	L	H	I	T
X	F	J	K	V	U	H	C	K	S	T	M	O	X
B	O	T	H	A	S	R	F	G	R	H	S	D	P
U	Z	X	V	B	E	N	M	A	F	J	A	F	G
T	C	I	C	P	R	F	E	X	B	K	L	T	L
T	Q	D	Y	A	Y	B	N	C	N	M	T	Y	E
O	I	J	L	K	R	T	J	D	O	Z	P	U	A
N	W	C	C	B	P	R	O	C	E	A	N	R	V
U	N	R	E	A	L	L	Y	S	A	Q	W	E	E
V	R	U	C	M	W	O	N	D	E	R	F	U	L

Vocabulary Words to Search For:

evaporate	really	percent
both	wonderful	enjoy
button	leave	salt
carry	mix	climb
ocean	earth	

B Action!

Do this with a small group of people. Each person takes a turn acting out a verb from the list below. The person to guess the correct verb wins and gets to "act out" the next action word.

Verbs:

carry   climb   enjoy   feed   leave   mix
move   destroy   travel   swim   breathe

Think of some more words to act out on your own.

Dictionary Page

Finding Compound Words in the Dictionary

1. You already know that *compound words* are made of two separate words. Sometimes these nouns have a space between them, and sometimes they are together.

   Examples: tour + guide = tour guide
   lamp + shade = lampshade

   Put the words on the left together with the words on the right to make as many compound nouns as you can. Use your dictionary for help.

2. Take five of your compound words from Part I and write them in alphabetical order. Next, look up the words in your dictionary. Write a sentence using each word.

   Example: *There are many kinds of plants and animals in the rain forest.*

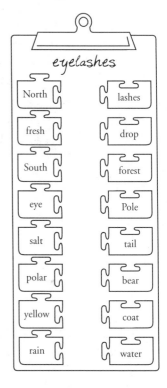

eyelashes

North	lashes
fresh	drop
South	forest
eye	Pole
salt	tail
polar	bear
yellow	coat
rain	water

a. _____

b. _____

c. _____

d. _____

e. _____

Plants

Context Clues

Choose the meaning of the boldface (dark) words. These words are in this unit. *Don't use your dictionary.*

1. Paul was born twenty-five years **ago.** He is 25 years old.
   a. again
   b. after today
   c. before now
   d. leave

2. We don't need these papers any more. Let's **burn** them.
   a. put them in the fire
   b. put them in the desk
   c. keep them
   d. store them

3. You can see beautiful pictures at an art **museum.** You can see things about science at a science **museum.** Most museums belong to the government.
   a. a building with beautiful and interesting things to look at
   b. a store that sells paintings and other beautiful things
   c. an aquarium or zoo
   d. a place where scientists work

4. Ann studied very hard for the test today. She is a good student. She will **probably** get a good grade.
   a. maybe
   b. cannot
   c. 50 percent sure
   d. almost 100 percent sure

5. You cannot drink most river water. If you drink it, you may get a **disease.**
   a. fish
   b. sickness
   c. sea animals
   d. thirsty

6. Cotton is an important **crop** in Egypt. Vegetables are an important **crop** in parts of Mexico. Coffee is an important **crop** in Brazil.
   a. plants that farmers grow
   b. plants near a house
   c. something a country buys from another country
   d. food that a farmer grows

7. The **soil** near the Nile River is very rich. There are also water and sun. There are many farms there and the plants grow very well.
    a. good clean water
    b. dirt or land
    c. sunshine
    d. fruit and vegetables

8. It is **around** 25°C (25 degrees Celsius) today.
    a. hot
    b. cold
    c. in a circle
    d. about

9. Many Brazilian farmers **raise** coffee on their farms.
    a. grow
    b. find
    c. pick up
    d. enjoy

10. There are streets in a city. There are roads between small towns. There are **highways** between important cities.
    a. up above
    b. large, wide roads
    c. small streets
    d. airplanes

11. It is 2:56. It is **nearly** 3:00.
    a. beside
    b. inside
    c. almost
    d. after

12. Tom is a mechanic. He works in a large garage. He **earns** $15.00 an hour.
    a. fixes cars
    b. gets money for work
    c. gets tired
    d. pays

13. Some plants are poisonous. The poison is **natural** in the plants. No one puts it there.
    a. something made by people
    b. something not made by people
    c. something in the ocean
    d. something on farms

The Date Palm

LESSON

Pre-reading Questions

1. What kind of trees are these?
2. Can you eat anything from these trees?
3. Do you have these trees near your city?

1

The Date Palm

The **date palm** is a wonderful tree. People eat dates. They feed them to their animals. They use the **leaves** and **wood** to build houses. They use the wood to build boats. They make
5 **baskets** from the leaves. They **burn** the other parts of the tree so they can cook food.

The date palm came from the Middle East. Seven thousand (7,000) years **ago,** people in Syria and Egypt ate dates. They made pic-
10 tures of date palms on their **stone** buildings. Today date palms grow in the Middle East, parts of Asia and Africa, **southern** Europe, and other warm parts of the world.

There are more than twenty-seven hun-
15 dred (2,700) kinds of palm trees. Most of them cannot grow in the Middle East because it is too dry. The date palm grows there very well.

Hundreds of years ago people in southern Europe and Arab countries made pictures of
20 palm trees and palm flowers on some of their buildings. Today we can see these pictures in **art museums.** People think that the palm tree is beautiful. People thought the same thing a long time ago.

leaf

before now

adjective for *south*

basket

A   Vocabulary

burn	date palm	southern	art
leaves	grow	wood	museums
ago	buildings	baskets	stone

1. Today we can see these pictures in _____ _____.
2. They use the _____ and _____ to build houses.
3. Today date palms grow in the Middle East, parts of Asia and Africa, _____ Europe, and other warm parts of the world.
4. The _____ is a wonderful tree.
5. They _____ the other parts of the tree so they can cook food.
6. Seven thousand years _____, people in Syria and Egypt ate dates.
7. They make _____ from the leaves.
8. They made pictures of date palms on their _____ buildings.

B   Vocabulary (new context)

southern	palm	burn	leaves
museum	wood	basket	art
think	ago	dates	stone

1. Some trees have very large green _____.
2. Argentina is in the _____ part of South America.
3. Marie started to study English five years _____.
4. Stone cannot _____. Wood can.
5. People burn _____ to make a fire.
6. A science _____ is a very interesting place.
7. There is a _____ of fruit on the table.
8. Pam has a small _____ in her shoe. It hurts.
9. One kind of _____ tree gives oil. People make soap from it.
10. People dry _____ and keep them for a long time.
11. Michelangelo was an artist. His _____ is very famous.

C Vocabulary Review

both	stars	difficult	so
hearing-impaired	each other	idea	whole
sign	interpreter	dance	heat
weigh	stomach	believe	could

1. An _____ speaks two languages.
2. Do you _____ that there are farms in the sea?
3. There are a lot of _____ out tonight. The sky is beautiful.
4. They _____ not come to the party last night. They were too busy.
5. How tall are you and how much do you _____?
6. Palm trees like the _____ but not the cold.
7. The _____ says "Please use other door."
8. A piano is a thing. Love is an _____.
9. The students usually talk to _____ between classes.
10. Bill cleaned his _____ apartment on Saturday.
11. The hippo has a very long _____.
12. Do you like to _____?

D Questions

1. How do people use the palm tree?
*2. What is the name of the fruit of the palm tree?
3. Where did the date palm come from?
4. When did Syrians and Egyptians start to eat dates?
5. How many kinds of palm trees are there?
6. Why can't most of them grow in the Middle East?
7. Where can we see beautiful old pictures of palm trees?
*8. Why did Syrians and Egyptians make pictures of palm trees?
*9. Why do date palms grow in the Middle East?

E Comprehension

1. People make boats from the ———— of palm trees.
   a. leaves   c. dates
   b. wood   d. flowers

2. They make baskets from the ————.
   a. leaves   c. dates
   b. wood   d. flowers

3. They ———— part of the tree to make a fire.
   a. enjoy   c. burn
   b. dance   d. grow

4. The date palm came from ————.
   a. California   c. southern Europe
   b. Africa   d. the Middle East

5. People started to grow date palms about ———— years ago.
   a. a few hundred   c. 5,000
   b. 100   d. 7,000

6. Date palms grow ————.
   a. in the land of the polar bear   c. where kiwis live
   b. in hot or warm places   d. in cool places

7. There are more than ———— kinds of palm trees.
   a. a few hundred   c. 2,000
   b. 100   d. 7,000

8. People use ———— palm tree.
   a. the whole   c. almost all of the
   b. the leaves and wood of the d. the fruit and leaves of the

F Main Idea

1. The date palm grows in the Middle East.
2. The date palm is beautiful, and people use all of it.
3. People made pictures of the date palm, and these pictures are in art museums now.

The Water Hyacinth

LESSON

2

Pre-reading Questions

1. Where does the water hyacinth grow?

2. How many water hyacinths do you see?

3. What are the people doing?

The Water Hyacinth

The **water hyacinth** grow in tropical countries. It has beautiful purple-blue flowers, but everybody **hates** it. Why?

≠ loves

5 Millions and millions of these plants grow in rivers and lakes. Sometimes the plants **become so** thick that people can walk on them. People cannot travel in boats on the water, and they cannot fish in it. The plants stop the water from moving. Then the water carries **diseases.**

sicknesses

10 Farmers cannot use the water on their land.

Now scientists think that water hyacinths can be useful. The plants are really a free **crop.** No one has to take care of them. They **just** grow and grow and grow. What can farmers use them for?

plants a farmer grows

15 Some fish like to eat them. Farmers can grow these fish in the lakes and rivers.

Workers can collect and cut the plants with **machines.** Then they can make **fertilizer** to make their crops grow **better.** They can also 20 make feed for their farm animals.

Maybe it will be possible to make **methane gas** (CH_4) for **energy.** (We burn gas from petroleum for energy. Methane gas comes from plants.) Then poor tropical countries will 25 not have to buy so much expensive petroleum.

Maybe in the future people will love the water hyacinth instead of hating it.

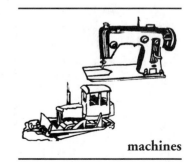

machines

A Vocabulary

feed	machines	energy	hates
water hyacinth	diseases	crop	millions
so	just	lakes	methane gas
become	better	fertilizer	petroleum

1. Workers can collect and cut the plants with _____.
2. Then they can make _____ to make their crops grow _____.
3. Maybe it will be possible to make _____ (CH$_4$) for _____.
4. It has beautiful purple-blue flowers, but everybody _____ it.
5. The plants are really a free _____.
6. Sometimes the plants _____ _____ thick that people can walk on them.
7. The _____ grows in tropical countries.
8. They _____ grow and grow and grow.

B Vocabulary (new context)

just	hate	tropical	disease
better	petroleum	become	lakes
travel	feed	fertilizer	energy
machines	crop	so	flowers

1. Rice is an important _____ in Asia.
2. Tom became very sick with a _____. He died.
3. A grade of 90% is _____ than 60%.
4. I am _____ tired that I can't study.
5. Patty is _____ a baby. She cannot walk
6. Farm _____ make the work easier.
7. Many farmers in China make their own _____.
8. Some students _____ to study. They just want to have a good time.
9. Mary wants to _____ an engineer.
10. We use gas and oil for _____.

C   Vocabulary Review

Match the words that mean the same.

Column A
1. also _____
2. difficult _____
3. modern _____
4. both _____
5. enjoy _____
6. toward _____
7. hearing-impaired _____
8. expensive _____
9. percent _____
10. group _____

Column B
a. two
b. can't hear well
c. not cheap
d. not easy
e. %
f. leaves
g. like
h. too
i. new
j. own
k. to
l. several

D   Questions

1. Where does the water hyacinth grow?
2. Why do people hate this plant? Tell three reasons.
3. Water hyacinths are a free crop. What does this mean?
4. How can people use water hyacinths? Tell four ways.
5. What is the difference between methane gas and other gas?
*6. Cheap energy is very important for poor countries. Why?

E   Comprehension

_____ 1. Water hyacinths grow very thick on some tropical lakes and rivers.

_____ 2. Sometimes the water under the plants cannot move.

_____ 3. Water hyacinths help make water clean.

_____ 4. Maybe farmers can use water hyacinths.

_____ *5. Water hyacinths grow in parts of Asia and Africa.

_____ 6. Some kinds of fish like to eat water hyacinths.

_____ 7. Water hyacinths can make petroleum.

_____ *8. These plants can give farmers more money.

F Main Idea

Match the details with the main ideas. Write the letter under the correct
main idea. Two details do not belong under a main idea.

1. People hate water hyacinths.   **2. Water hyacinths can be useful.**

a. Some fish like to eat them.
b. The plants stop the water from moving.
c. People cannot travel on the water.
d. People can make fertilizer out of them.
e. Maybe people can make methane gas.
f. They have beautiful flowers.
g. People can feed them to animals.
h. We burn gas from petroleum for energy.
i. People cannot fish.
j. The water carries diseases.

Rice

LESSON

3

Pre-reading Questions

1. What is the person doing?
2. Where does rice grow?
3. Do you eat rice? When? Do you like it?

Rice

People all over the world eat **rice.** Millions of people in Asia, Africa, and South America eat it every day of their lives. Some people eat almost nothing but rice.

5   Rice is a kind of **grass.** There are more than seven thousand (7,000) kinds of rice. Most kinds are water plants. Farmers grow rice in many countries, **even** in the southern part of the United States and in **eastern** Australia.

10   No one really knows where rice came from. Some scientists think it started to grow in two places. They think that one kind of rice grew in southern Asia thousands of years ago. Someone in China wrote about it almost five

15 thousand (5,000) years ago. Another kind **probably** grew in <u>West</u> Africa. Other scientists think rice came from India, and Indian travelers took it to other parts of the world.

    There are two main ways to grow rice.

20 Upland rice grows in dry <u>soil.</u> Most rice grows in wet soil. People in many countries do all of the work by hand. This is the same way farmers worked hundreds of years ago. Some countries now use machines on their rice farms. The

25 farmers all use fertilizer. Some <u>insects</u> are enemies of rice. Farmers poison them.

insects

rug

sandals

land, dirt

broom

People use every part of the rice plant. They make animal feed and rice oil from it. They also make baskets, **brooms, rugs, sandals,** and **roofs**
30 for their houses. They burn dry rice plants for cooking.

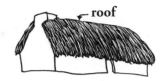

A Vocabulary

brooms	grass	probably	West
rice	rugs	eastern	soil
sandals	even	roofs	insects

1. They also make baskets, _____, _____, _____, and _____ for their houses.
2. Rice is a kind of _____.
3. People all over the world eat _____.
4. Farmers grow rice in many countries, _____ in the southern part of the United States and in _____ Australia.
5. Some _____ are enemies of rice.
6. Another kind _____ grew in _____ Africa.
7. Upland rice grows in dry _____.

B Vocabulary (new context)

even	probably	rice	eastern
rug	sandals	grass	insects
roof	soil	West	broom

1. In the summer people like to wear _____ instead of shoes.
2. Chicken, _____, and salad make a good dinner.
3. Frank is two years old. He wants to play basketball, but he can't _____ pick up the ball.
4. We can have our picnic on the _____ under that tree.
5. Paul cleaned the garage floor with a _____.
6. The rain comes through the _____ of the old house.
7. Korea is in the _____ part of Asia.

8. Some _____ live together in a group.
9. Lebanon is in _____ Asia.
10. There are a lot of black clouds in the sky. It will _____ rain.
11. Plants must have sun, water, and good _____ .
12. Mr. and Mrs. Cook have a beautiful new _____ for the living room floor.

C Vocabulary Review

Match the words that mean the opposite.

Column A
1. already _____
2. large _____
3. toward _____
4. enemy _____
5. difficult _____
6. hate _____
7. cheap _____
8. collect _____
9. heat _____
10. southern _____

Column B
a. easy
b. cold
c. not yet
d. northern
e. small
f. friend
g. each other
h. away from
i. pass out
j. wood
k. expensive
l. love

D Questions

*1. Why do some people eat almost nothing but rice?
*2. In what countries is rice an important food?
3. What kind of plant is rice?
4. How many kinds of rice are there?
5. Scientists have two ideas about where rice came from. What are they?
*6. What does "upland" mean?
*7. Why do rice farmers use fertilizer?
*8. Why do most farmers grow rice by hand?
9. How do farmers kill insects?
10. People eat rice. Tell other ways people use the rice plant.

E Comprehension: True/False/No Information

———— 1. Rice is a kind of grass.
———— 2. Rice grows on dry land and in wet soil.
———— 3. Scientists know that rice came from India.
———— 4. Rice grows in the United States.
———— 5. There are more than 7,000 kinds of rice.
———— 6. Maybe Chinese travelers took rice to India.
———— 7. More people grow rice with machines than by hand.
———— 8. Farmers use fertilizer to kill insects.
———— 9. Chinese farms need more fertilizer than Indian farms.
———— 10. People use every part of the rice plant.

F Main Idea

1. Rice is a very important crop, but nobody knows where it came from.
2. People grow rice in many countries.
3. Today rice farmers use machines, fertilizer, and poisons.

Oranges

LESSON

Pre-reading Questions

1. What is the man doing?
2. What can you do with oranges?
3. Do oranges grow in your country?

Oranges

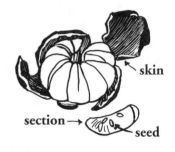

Everybody loves oranges. They are **sweet** and juicy. They are in **sections** so it is easy to eat them. Some oranges do not have any **seeds.** Some have a thick **skin** and some have a **thin** skin.

5   The orange tree is beautiful. It has a lot of **shiny** green leaves. The small white flowers smell very sweet. An orange tree has flowers and fruit at the same time.

There were orange trees twenty million 10   years ago. The oranges were very small, not like the ones today. The orange tree probably came from China. Many different kinds of **wild** oranges grow there today. Chinese started to **raise** orange trees **around** 2400 B.C. Chinese 15   art has **lovely** old pictures of oranges and orange trees.

not planted by people

raise = grow/around = about

Farmers in other parts of Asia and the Middle East learned to raise oranges from the Chinese. Then they taught Europeans. The 20   Spanish planted orange trees in the New World (North and South America). They took them to Florida first. Oranges are a very important crop in Florida today.

"Orange" is both a fruit and a color. The 25   color of oranges is so beautiful that in English we use the name of the fruit for the color.

A Vocabulary

around	wild	sections	lovely
skin	oranges	raise	smell
seeds	shiny	thin	sweet

1. Chinese started to _____ orange trees _____ 2400 B.C.
2. They are _____ and juicy.
3. Some have a thick _____ and some have a _____ skin.
4. Many different kinds of _____ oranges grow there today.
5. They are in _____ so it is easy to eat them.
6. Chinese art has _____ old pictures of oranges and orange trees.
7. Some oranges do not have any _____.
8. It has a lot of _____ green leaves.

B Vocabulary (new context)

orange	lovely	sweet	wild
sections	raise	shines	leaves
seeds	around	thin	skin

1. Japanese _____ fish on farms in the sea.
2. The Syrians made _____ pictures of date palms on stone buildings.
3. Plants grow from _____.
4. A bird has feathers on its _____. A camel has hair.
5. The polar bear and hippo are _____ animals.
6. There are three _____ of the beginning class.
7. The sun _____ every day in the desert.
8. Dates and oranges are _____.
9. Carlos is fat. Pablo is _____.
10. People started eating dates _____ 7,000 years ago.

C Vocabulary Review

interpreter	museums	become	better
diseases	energy	gas	grass
west	east	broom	roof
even	insects	sandals	soil

1. Sweden is ——————— of Norway and ——————— of Finland.
2. Students always ——————— very busy at the end of the semester.
3. Many kinds of ——————— eat farmers' crops.
4. The Whites have ——————— all around their house. There are also flowers and trees.
5. Desert ——————— is very dry.
6. We can get some ——————— from drinking dirty water.
7. Tom looked everywhere for his dictionary. He ——————— looked in his car.
8. Roberto is an ———————. He works in Geneva.
9. Tourists usually go to art ——————— to see beautiful pictures.
10. Your feet feel cool when you wear ———————.
11. Lois is a ——————— student than Helen. Helen is not a good student.
12. The ——————— is on the outside of the house. The ceiling is on the inside.

D Questions

1. Describe an orange.
2. Do all oranges have seeds?
3. Describe an orange tree.
4. Where did the orange tree probably come from?
5. Who plants wild orange trees?
6. How did Europeans learn to raise oranges?
7. How did the United States get orange trees?
8. What does "orange" mean?
*9. Why did people in Saudi Arabia eat dates instead of oranges?

E Comprehension

1. Oranges are _____.
   a. shiny and green   c. sweet and juicy
   b. old and wild   d. thin and white

2. Some oranges do not have _____.
   a. seeds   c. flowers
   b. sections   d. a skin

3. Orange leaves are _____.
   a. shiny   c. sweet
   b. thick   d. wild

4. There are many _____ orange trees in China today.
   a. shiny   c. wild
   b. thin   d. thick

5. Europeans learned to plant orange trees from farmers in _____.
   a. the Middle East and Asia   c. China
   b. Florida   d. Spain

*6. Oranges do not grow in _____.
   a. India   c. Mexico
   b. Sweden   d. North Africa

F Main Idea

1. Oranges are sweet and juicy with seeds and a skin.
2. Orange trees went from Asia to the Middle East to Europe to the New World.
3. Oranges probably came from China, and today people all over the world like them because they are sweet and juicy.

Guayule

← rubber tree

guayule

LESSON

5

Pre-reading Questions

1. What is guayule?

2. What is the person doing?

3. Why are a rubber tree and a guayule in the same picture?

Guayule

Rubber is very important in the modern world. We use it for **tires** for automobiles, buses, **trucks, motorcycles,** and airplanes. We use large trucks and other machines to build
5 **highways.** They have large rubber tires.

Natural rubber comes from trees. Most of the world's rubber comes from Malaysia, Indonesia, and Thailand in Southeast Asia. We also make rubber from petroleum. This kind of
10 rubber becomes hot very fast. We can use it for only some kinds of tires.

Now scientists can make rubber from **guayule.** This wild plant grows in northern Mexico and the southwestern United States. It
15 doesn't need very much rain. It can grow in desert soil. Guayule rubber is **nearly** the same as rubber from the rubber tree.

Native Americans in Arizona **plan** to start guayule farms. They know a lot about farming
20 in the desert. The farms will use poor desert land and give people **jobs.** The Native Americans think they can make a lot of money from guayule rubber.

Poor desert countries in Africa could grow
25 guayule too. People could **earn** money on their own desert land. If they grow their own rubber, they will not have to buy it from other countries.

tires

truck

almost

motorcycle

work

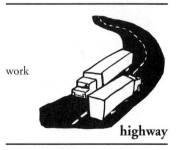

highway

A Vocabulary

natural	earn	jobs	Native Americans
guayule	tires	nearly	plan
rubber	motorcycles	trucks	highways

1. _____ rubber comes from trees.
2. We use it for _____ for automobiles, buses, _____, _____, and airplanes.
3. People could _____ money on their own desert land.
4. Now scientists can make rubber from _____.
5. We use large trucks and other machines to build _____.
6. _____ in Arizona _____ to start guayule farms.
7. Guayule rubber is _____ the same as rubber from the rubber tree.
8. _____ is very important in the modern world.
9. The farms will use poor desert land and give people _____.

B Vocabulary (new context)

rubber	tire	naturally	nearly
southwestern	earn	plan	motorcycle
truck	job	highways	Native Americans

1. Antonia works for the government. She doesn't _____ very much money.
2. Glen drives a _____. He is a truck driver.
3. It is _____ time for dinner.
4. My car needs a new _____.
5. Children like to play with a _____ ball.
6. What do you _____ to study after you learn English?
7. Some students have a part-time _____. They earn a little money.
8. Most countries have good _____ around the capital city.
9. George had a bicycle. Now he has a _____. Next he wants to buy a car.
10. Sea water is _____ salty. No one puts salt in it.
11. _____ live in all states of the United States of America.

C Vocabulary Review

Underline the word that does not belong.

1. oranges, water hyacinth, dates, rice
2. driver, interpreter, farmer, cheaper
3. burn, enjoy, have fun, like
4. cloud, moon, star, sun
5. wood, gas, stone, oil
6. south, east, west, northern
7. sugar, date, orange, rice
8. wild, wonderful, beautiful, lovely
9. broom, machine, roof, sandals
10. leaves, flowers, fruit, insects

D Questions

1. What do we use rubber for?
2. Where does natural rubber come from?
3. What countries grow most of the world's rubber?
4. Some rubber is made from petroleum. Why can't we use it for all kinds of tires?
5. Where does guayule grow wild?
*6. What is the land like there?
7. Who is going to grow guayule on farms in Arizona?
8. How will the farms help the Native Americans?
9. What other countries could grow guayule?
10. Why is it good for desert countries in Africa to grow their own rubber?
*11. Why does the modern world use a lot of rubber?
*12. Rubber trees don't grow in Europe. Why?
*13. Do Africans understand desert farming?

E Comprehension: True/False/No Information

_____ 1. Rubber grows in Sri Lanka and India.
_____ 2. Bicycles have rubber tires.
_____ 3. Motorcycles have rubber tires.
_____ 4. All rubber comes from trees.

_____　5. Rubber trees have shiny leaves.
_____　6. Guayule is a desert plant that grows in North America.
_____　7. Guayule is nearly the same as a water hyacinth.
_____　8. There are a lot of Native Americans in Arizona.
_____　9. Guayule needs rich soil and lots of water.
_____ 10. Guayule farms could make jobs for people.

F Main Idea

1. We can get rubber from guayule instead of rubber trees.
2. Guayule grows in northern Mexico and the southwestern United States.
3. Rubber is important in modern life.

Word Study

A Past Tense

Add **-ed** to most verbs for the past tense. If the verb ends in **e**, just add **-d.**

smell – smelled	raise – raised
earn – earned	hate – hated

Use the **y** rules. (See page 27.)

study – studied	play – played

Use the (one - one - one) (1-1-1) rule. (See page 28.)

plan – planned	shop – shopped

Some verbs are irregular. You must memorize them.

Simple	Past	Simple	Past	Simple	Past
come	came	eat	ate	grow	grew
make	made	become	became	think	thought
teach	taught	take	took	be	was, were

Put the past tense of the verb in each sentence.

(eat)　　　1. We _____ lunch at 1:00 yesterday.

(plan)　　　2. This morning Jeff _____ his whole day.

(take)　　　3. Ms. Sanchez _____ her daughter to the doctor yesterday.

(be)　　　4. Paul _____ nearly late for class this morning.

(carry)　　　5. Robert _____ his baggage into the airport.

(think)　　　6. We _____ about the problem for a long time last week.

(come)　　　7. Alice _____ to our party last Saturday.

(teach)　　　8. Mr. Hall _____ in Japan for six years. Now he teaches in New York.

(become)　　　9. Paula studied at the university for eight years. Last year she _____ a doctor.

(grow)　　　10. The Larsons _____ cotton on their land for ten years. Now they grow guayule.

(shop) 11. Jim _____ for three hours last night.

(make) 12. Donna _____ a chocolate cake yesterday.

(dance) 13. The students _____ a long time at the party last Friday night.

B Comparisons

We add **-er** to short adjectives (words with one syllable) to compare two things. We use **than**. We use **more than** with most longer words (words with three or more syllables).

> Example: Sally is **more beautiful than** Ann.
> Rice is **more important than** potatoes in China.

> Irregular: **good - better**   **bad - worse**   **far - farther**
>
> A car is **better than** a bicycle.
> A bicycle is **worse than** a car.
> An airplane can go **farther than** a car.

Write the correct form of the adjective. Then write *than*.

> Example: (interesting) New York is **more interesting than** Chicago.

(expensive) 1. A car is _____ a motorcycle.

(sweet) 2. Sugar is _____ oranges.

(good) 3. Oranges are _____ than grapefruit.

(thin) 4. Bill is _____ Paul.

(difficult) 5. French is _____ Spanish.

(small) 6. A date is _____ an orange.

(intelligent) 7. Ruth is _____ Lee.

(wonderful) 8. A trip to the moon is _____ a trip to the supermarket.

(far) 9. If you are in New York, Dallas is _____ than Chicago.

C Plural Nouns

Most of the rules for adding **-s** to nouns are the same as the rules for adding **-s** to verbs.

baby - babies	bus - buses
highway - highways	lunch - lunches

If a noun ends in **f,** change the **f** to **v** and add **-es.** If a noun ends in **fe,** change the **f** to **v** and add **-s.**

leaf – leaves   life – lives

Irregular: roof – roofs

Write the plural for each noun.

1. lunch _____
2. roof _____
3. knife _____
4. key _____
5. leaf _____
6. sandal _____
7. day _____
8. dress _____

9. crop _____
10. seed _____
11. family _____
12. aquarium _____
13. enemy _____
14. tire _____
15. match _____
16. library _____

D -y Adjectives

Add **-y** to some nouns or verbs to make an adjective.

cloud - cloudy   sun - sunny

Use the **1-1-1** rule.

sun - sunny   **But:** snow - snowy

If the word ends in **e,** drop the **e** and add **-y.**

shine - shiny   ice - icy

(See exercise on following page.)

Add -y to each word. Be careful of the spelling. Then choose the right word for each sentence.

salt	snow	juice	sun
ice	cloud	wind	shine

1. Yesterday was a beautiful day. It was _____. The sky is _____ today. The weather is bad.
2. Oranges are _____. Bananas are not.
3. Gold is _____.
4. In winter there are often _____ days. Sometimes the streets become _____.
5. In spring there are _____ days. The wind blows a lot.
6. This food is too _____. I can't eat it.

E **Writing**

Write real information in your answers.

1. Which plant in *Unit 3* is the most useful in your opinion? Why?
2. Which plants in *Unit 3* can you find in your country? Why?
3. Which plant in *Unit 3* is the most beautiful in your opinion? Why?

Video Highlights

A Before You Watch

1. Circle Cameroon on this map.

2. Discuss these questions with your classmates.
   - Why are plants important to humans and animals?
   - Why do people cut down forests?
3. Read this helpful information before you watch the video.

   Bakas—a group of people who live in the rain forests of Cameroon. There are about 40,000 Bakas in Cameroon. Another name for the Bakas is "Pygmies."
   Bantus—a large group of people who live in central Africa and speak the same language. There are about 15,000,000 Bantus in Cameroon.
   ethnic group—a group of people who share the same culture and language. A country may have many different ethnic groups.

©CNN

B   As You Watch

Finish this sentence with at least two more reasons.

The forest is important to the Bakas because . . .

1. *the people love the land.*

2. _____

3. _____

C   After You Watch

1. True, False, or No Information (NI)?
   a. ____ The Bakas do not know how to live in the forest.
   b. ____ The Bakas make poison from plants to kill their enemies.
   c. ____ The Bakas use plants from the forest for food and medicine.
   d. ____ Most of the people in Cameroon are Bantus.

2. Comprehension/Discussion Questions
   a. Who are the enemies of the Bakas? Why?
   b. What happens to the Bakas when they leave the forest? What are the good things? What are the bad things?

Activity Page

A Unscramble the Words

What do people use to make these products? Unscramble the words on the left to find out.

Example:

EDTA SAMPL

DATE PALMS _____

Baskets are made from these kinds of trees.

1. ODWO

_____

People use this to build houses, furniture, and boats.

2. CREI

_____

Brooms, rugs, sandals, and roofs can all be made from parts of this plant.

3. BERRUB

_____

This can be used to make tires for trucks, motorcycles, and other large machines.

4. YLUAEGU

_____

Scientists can now make rubber from this plant.

B Look Around the Room

Play this game with a partner.

Partner A: Look around the room. Make a list of all the things that come from plants. Give the list to your partner.

Partner B: Go and touch each thing on the list, one by one. Tell your partner what plant it comes from. Write the name of the plant on the list.

Example: *table*   *tree*

Read your list aloud to your classmates. Which team of students found the most things?

Dictionary Page

Finding the Correct Spelling

1. Make a sentence using the past tense of each of these verbs. Be sure to follow the spelling rules and watch out for irregular verbs!

   Example:

   carry   *The woman <u>carried</u> the food out of the forest in a large basket.*

   dance   _____

   see   _____

   make   _____

   swim   _____

   raise   _____

   become   _____

   earn   _____

   catch   _____

   Look up these verbs in your dictionary to make sure that you spelled each one correctly.

2. Add *-y* to nouns and verbs below to make adjectives. When you are finished, use your dictionary to check your work.

   Example: star *<u>starry</u>*

   smell _____   grass _____

   salt _____   rubber _____

   Now try using two of these new adjectives in sentences of your own.

   Example: *It was a beautiful, <u>starry</u> night.*

   _____

   _____

Popular Music

Context Clues

These words are in this unit.

1. Sarah is in the hospital. I plan to **visit** her this afternoon.
    a. help
    b. go to see
    c. hate
    d. drive to her house

2. Most rice grows in water or wet soil. **However,** some rice grows on dry land.
    a. and
    b. so
    c. if
    d. but

3. The class finishes at 10:50. It is 10:45 now, and the class will finish **soon.**
    a. tomorrow
    b. later
    c. in a short time
    d. early

4. Cola drinks are **popular** all over the world.
    a. people like them
    b. natural
    c. people hate them
    d. possible

5. People started to make things with machines during the **century** from 1800 to 1900.
    a. ten years
    b. fifty years
    c. a hundred years
    d. a thousand years

6. When you **add** two and two, you get four.
    a. +
    b. –
    c. x
    d. ÷

7. This is a poor movie. It is very slow and **boring.**
    a. good
    b. not interesting
    c. not fast
    d. lovely

8. Mr. Baker has his own **company**. The company sells fruit and vegetables to supermarkets.
    a. business
    b. motorcycle
    c. car
    d. job

9. Oscar usually listens to the car radio **while** he drives to class.
   a. after
   b. before
   c. when
   d. but

10. Bill and Paul planned to go to Europe together. Then Bill got sick so Paul went **alone.**
    a. He didn't go.
    b. He wanted to go.
    c. No one went with him.
    d. He went with Bill.

Classical Music

LESSON

1

Pre-reading Questions

1. What kind of music are they playing?
2. What is the person in front doing?
3. Do you like classical music?

1

Classical Music

All over the world people listen to **classical** music. Classical music is difficult to describe. It means different things to different people.

Some famous classical **composers** were Bach, *music writers*
5 Vivaldi, Haydn, and Mozart. In their music, they did not tell a story or show **strong emotion.** They wanted to make a beautiful, interesting **design.** They wanted to write lovely sounds.

Then composers started to interpret ideas.
10 They told stories about **wars, armies,** and **soldiers.** They wrote about **religion.** Sometimes they composed music for **holidays.** They told love stories and showed strong emotion. Some of these composers were Beethoven, Schumann,
15 Chopin, Mendelssohn, Wagner, and Tchaikovsky.

Classical music stays with people a long time. Bach wrote about 300 years ago, Beethoven wrote about 200 years ago, and Tchaikovsky wrote over 100 years ago.

20 Sometimes people close their eyes to listen to classical music. When they close their eyes, they can see the design. They can listen to the same classical music many times and enjoy it. Sometimes it is difficult to understand. The lis-
25 tener has to think about it. **However,** we can *but* all learn to enjoy some classical music. It is very important to people.

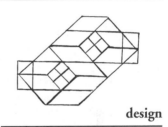

design

soldier

A   Vocabulary

wars	religion	armies	however
holidays	soldiers	around	strong
classical	even	composers	emotion
design	energy	crop	both

1. Some famous classical _____ were Bach, Vivaldi, Haydn, and Mozart.
2. They wanted to make a beautiful, interesting _____.
3. They wrote about _____.
4. Sometimes they composed music for _____.
5. They told stories about _____, _____, and _____.
6. In their music, they did not tell a story or show _____ _____.
7. _____, we can all learn to enjoy some classical music.
8. All over the world people listen to _____ music.

B   Vocabulary (new context)

War	religion	army	however
holiday	soldier	different	strong
classical	listen	composer	emotions
design	energy	crop	both

1. Ali is a Muslim. This is his _____. Maria is a Christian.
2. We can make rubber from petroleum. _____, we cannot use it for all kinds of tires.
3. The Second World _____ started in 1939 and ended in 1945.
4. Bob was in the _____ for four years. He was a _____.
5. Some people go to sleep when they hear _____ music.
6. Today the schools, banks, and offices are closed. No one is going to work because today is a _____.
7. Leonard Bernstein wrote a lot of popular music. He was a famous _____.
8. I cannot drink this coffee because it is too _____.
9. From the air, the city lights make a beautiful _____.
10. Love and hate are _____.

C Vocabulary Review

truck	job	rubber	natural
plan	skin	sections	palm
earth	mixed	evaporates	freshwater
music	only	weighs	stomach

1. Helen has a new ——————————. She will work at the university.
2. Seats in some —————————— of the stadium are expensive.
3. The Jensens —————————— to go to Japan next summer.
4. Pat's hair is not really blond. The —————————— color is brown.
5. The moon travels around the —————————— once every twenty-four hours.
6. If you leave water out in the sun, it ——————————.
7. Food stays in your —————————— for several hours.
8. Students from different countries are —————————— together in the same class.
9. Some —————————— fish live in very cold water.
10. A hippopotamus —————————— more than a camel.
11. You can hear —————————— on the radio twenty-four hours a day.
12. People from different parts of the world have different color ——————————.

D Questions

1. Where is classical music famous?
2. What did Bach want to do in his music?
3. Name two composers who told stories and showed strong emotion.
4. Why do people sometimes close their eyes when they listen to classical music?
5. When did Tchaikovsky write his music?
6. What kinds of stories did some composers tell in their music?
7. Is classical music always easy to understand?
*8. Why is classical music important to people?

E Comprehension

1. Bach composed his music _____ years ago.
   a. thousands of
   b. over 500
   c. about 300
   d. fifty

2. Vivaldi wanted to _____.
   a. make a design
   b. show strong emotion
   c. tell a love story
   d. tell a story about war

3. The first classical composers wanted to _____.
   a. tell stories about religion
   b. make an interesting design
   c. write lovely sounds
   d. b and c

4. Tchaikovsky _____.
   a. did not tell stories
   b. wrote 200 years ago
   c. showed emotion
   d. a and b

5. Haydn composed _____.
   a. love stories
   b. stories about armies
   c. classical music
   d. ideas

6. Some people enjoy _____ classical music.
   a. smelling
   b. listening to
   c. growing
   d. feeding

Blues and Jazz

LESSON

2

Pre-reading Questions

1. What are the men doing?

2. How are the two men different from each other?

3. Do you play any kind of music?

Blues and Jazz

People from Europe and America brought Africans to America as **slaves** before and during the nineteenth **century.** These Africans brought their music with them. After the American Civil

5 War (1861–1865), the African-American people in the United States were not slaves. Their African-American music became famous. It started in the South, in Louisiana and Mississippi. Then it traveled to the North. This music became

10 **blues** and then **jazz.**

Blues and jazz became very **popular** in the twentieth century. A person who "sings the blues" feels sad. Usually, he or she lost something—a person or maybe money or a job.

15 Blues **express** sad **feelings,** sometimes in a funny way. People played blues first with only one or two **instruments,** for example, a **guitar,** a **harmonica,** or sometimes a piano. Sometimes they sang without any instruments. Some

20 famous blues musicians are Bessie Smith, John Lee Hooker, and B. B. King. B. B. King named his guitar "Lucille."

Jazz came **soon** after blues. Composers **added** more musical instruments. Jazz can be happier and

25 is often faster. Some famous jazz musicians are Duke Ellington, Louis Armstrong, Miles Davis, and Wynton Marsalis.

---

100 years

guitar

---

many people like it

---

express = say or tell/
feelings = emotions

harmonica

---

soon = in a short time/
added = put in, +

Musicians who play blues and jazz change the music to show their emotions. They play the music differently each time. Today people all over the world still like to listen to blues and jazz because all people have strong emotional feelings sometimes.

A Vocabulary

century	popular	added	soon
listen	design	express	guitar
usually	instruments	slaves	harmonica
feelings	blues	jazz	sections

1. This music became _____ and then _____.
2. People from Europe and America brought Africans to America as _____ before and during the nineteenth _____.
3. Blues and jazz became very _____ in the twentieth century.
4. People played blues first with only one or two _____, for example, a _____, a _____, or sometimes a piano.
5. Jazz came _____ after blues.
6. Blues _____ sad _____, sometimes in a funny way.
7. Composers _____ more musical instruments.

B Vocabulary (new context)

century	popular	add	soon
listen	design	express	guitar
usually	instrument	slaves	harmonica
feel	blues	jazz	sections

1. There are one hundred years in a _____.
2. You play the _____ with your hands.

3. You play the _____ with your mouth.
4. Can you _____ these numbers? 456 + 142 + 862 = ?
5. Some people _____ their emotions by crying or laughing.
6. If you _____ happy, you laugh.
7. John Lee Hooker sings the _____, and Wynton Marsalis plays _____.
8. The piano is a musical _____.
9. The dolphin is a _____ animal at an aquarium.
10. Keiko will finish her English course _____. She will finish it in two weeks.
11. _____ worked on American farms in the nineteenth century.

C Vocabulary Review

Match the words that mean the same.

Column A

1. composer _____
2. however _____
3. listen _____
4. soldier _____
5. natural _____
6. lovely _____
7. thin _____
8. rice _____
9. highway _____
10. roof _____
11. sandal _____
12. earn _____
13. war _____

Column B

a. someone in the army
b. the top of a house
c. not made by people
d. get money for work
e. a writer of music
f. hear
g. picture
h. beautiful
i. fighting
j. a wide road
k. not fat
l. smell
m. an important food for some people
n. but
o. a kind of shoe

D Questions

1. Why did European and American people bring Africans to America before and during the nineteenth century?
2. Where did blues and jazz start?
3. When did blues and jazz become very popular?
4. How does a person who "sings the blues" feel?
*5. When do you feel like singing the blues?
6. With what instruments did people first play the blues?
7. What is the name of B. B. King's guitar?
*8. Why do you think B. B. King gave his guitar a name?
*9. What is the difference between jazz and blues?
10. Why are blues and jazz popular all over the world?

E Comprehension: True/False

_____ *1. Blues and jazz come from African music.
_____ 2. The American Civil War ended in 1865.
_____ 3. Jazz and blues started in the southern part of Europe.
_____ 4. A person who "sings the blues" feels happy because he found something.
_____ *5. If someone gives you a million dollars, you will sing the blues.
_____ 6. People can sing the blues with no instruments.
_____ 7. John Lee Hooker is a famous blues musician.
_____ 8. Jazz is sometimes happier music than blues.
_____ 9. Musicians play jazz and blues the same way each time.

Rock and Roll

LESSON

3

Pre-reading Questions

1. Who is the person on the left?

2. Look at the person on the right. Do you like the way he is dressed? Do you know a person who dresses that way?

3. Do you like rock and roll music? If so, who is your favorite artist?

Rock and Roll

Rock and roll came from jazz and blues during the 1950s. One of the first rock and roll songs was Bill Haley's "Rock Around the Clock." One of the first very famous rock and roll singers was Elvis

5 Presley. Others were Buddy Holly and Chuck Berry. Now, almost every country has many rock and roll **bands** and singers. Sometimes **performers** call their music by different names, like "rap" or "punk." They sing and play **mixtures** of rock

10 and roll and talking or other sounds. "Rap" and "punk" both came from rock and roll, or "rock music."

Some **fans** who like rock music think classical music is **boring.** Many fans play rock

15 music very loudly. They forget about the people who enjoy **soft** music. Loud music can make these people **nervous.** Many fans also like to dance to rock and roll.

When rock and roll was new, people had

20 only **records** to play the music at home. After that, we used cassette tapes and records. Now, we listen to music on **compact discs.** Most modern bands and singers use **companies** to make **videos** of their songs. With videos, fans

25 can see the performers at the same time they listen to the music. Making a recording and the video that goes with it is very expensive.

record

noun for *mix*

not interesting

≠ loud

compact disc

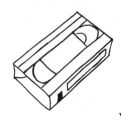

video

A   Vocabulary

boring	records	nervous	cassettes
composers	ago	mixtures	companies
baskets	raise	bands	compact discs
performers	videos	fans	soft

1. Most modern bands and singers use _____ to make _____ of their songs.
2. Some _____ who like rock music think classical music is _____.
3. They forget about the people who enjoy _____ music.
4. Loud music can make these people _____.
5. Now, almost every country has many rock and roll _____ and singers.
6. When rock and roll was new, people had only _____ to play the music at home.
7. Now, we listen to music on _____.
8. Sometimes _____ call their music by different names, like "rap" or "punk."
9. They sing and play _____ of rock and roll and talking or other sounds.

B   Vocabulary (new context)

soft	company	nervous	boring
mixture	records	cassettes	compact discs
raise	baskets	band	videos
performer	fan	ago	listen

1. Hot chocolate is a _____ of chocolate, sugar, and milk.
2. Ahmed works for a large _____ in Riyadh.
3. It is _____ to memorize vocabulary.
4. Students are usually _____ before a big test.
5. You can rent _____ at some stores and watch them at home.
6. Are you a _____ of rock and roll or classical music?
7. A famous _____ played at Laura's wedding.

8. _____ are more expensive than tapes.
9. You can play _____ only at home, not in your car.
10. Elvis Presley was a wonderful _____.
11. Loud music is not good for our ears, but _____ music is better.

C Vocabulary Review

Match the words that mean the opposite.

Column A
1. usually _____
2. thin _____
3. holiday _____
4. different _____
5. during _____
6. store _____
7. west _____
8. all over _____
9. spend _____
10. warm _____
11. somebody _____

Column B
a. east
b. earn
c. century
d. never
e. fat
f. work day
g. throw away
h. after
i. nowhere
j. slave
k. same
l. cool
m. popular
n. nobody

D Questions

1. What are "rap" and "punk"?
*2. Who was Bill Haley?
3. Where did rock and roll come from?
*4. Why do some rock and roll fans think classical music is boring?
5. In the 1950s, what did people use to play rock and roll at home?
6. Why do some fans like videos better than cassettes or compact discs?
7. Is it cheap to make a video?
8. Some people don't like loud music. Why?
9. Who were Elvis Presley, Buddy Holly, and Chuck Berry?
*10. Why does almost every country have many rock bands and singers?

E Comprehension

1. Many rock and roll fans like to _____ to the music.
   a. dance
   b. collect
   c. listen
   d. a and c

2. Bill Haley's "Rock Around the Clock" was one of the first _____ songs.
   a. blues
   b. rap
   c. rock and roll
   d. punk

3. "Rap" is a _____ of rock and roll and talking.
   a. mixture
   b. record
   c. performer
   d. company

4. Many fans like their rock music _____.
   a. soft
   b. nervous
   c. loud
   d. boring

5. Rock and roll came _____ classical music.
   a. before
   b. after
   c. during
   d. instead of

6. The first rock and roll fans listened to "Rock Around the Clock" on a _____.
   a. video
   b. cassette
   c. compact disc
   d. record

7. Elvis Presley was a famous _____.
   a. performer
   b. a and d
   c. band
   d. singer

8. Rock and roll began about _____ years ago.
   a. ten
   b. one hundred
   c. forty
   d. twenty-five

Country Western Music

LESSON

Pre-reading Questions

1. Why does the person on the left look like a cowboy?

2. Do you like country western music?

3. Do you know how to dance to country western music?

4

Country Western Music

<u>**Country**</u> western music is very old. It came from the United States, Canada, Ireland, and Great Britain. Country western music is a mixture of music from all of these places.

5   In the American West, cowboys had to take care of the <u>**cattle.**</u> They had to watch them all day and all night because the cattle were nervous and sometimes ran away. A cowboy's life was lonely and **dangerous.** When he was **alone** in

10   the desert with the cattle, he drank strong coffee with lots of **caffeine** to stay awake at night. He also sang music to the cattle to <u>**calm**</u> them. He sang about the stars and the moon, about his family and his friends. The cattle listened to the

15   cowboy and went to sleep. They did not run away if he sang beautiful, **peaceful** music.

The cowboys also sang music when they traveled to town to **relax** and have a good time. Sometimes they played **either** guitars or har-

20   monicas. Later, they used <u>**violins**</u> and other instruments.

In the American South, many people came from Ireland, Scotland, and England. Other people came from French Canada. They

25   enjoyed their own kind of music. They used guitars, violins, and harmonicas, too. They also

country

make them quiet

cattle

violin

added instruments from their homes, like **bottles, cans,** and spoons. When they **visited** their friends and families on holidays like **Thanksgiving,** they usually sang and played country music.

Country western music describes life. It talks about love, jobs, home, and money. It talks about friends and enemies, trucks and highways, farms and crops. People in many parts of the world like country western music because everyone knows something about these ideas. Also, many country western music fans wear western clothes and dance together to country western music. Many bands all over the world now perform country western music. Country western music fans enjoy Patsy Cline, Hank Williams, Loretta Lynn, and Randy Travis.

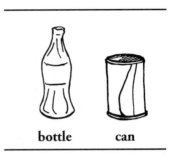

bottle   can

A Vocabulary

dangerous	bottles	caffeine	pieces
either	peaceful	cans	visited
alone	hotel	violins	calm
Thanksgiving	relax	cattle	country

1. When he was _____ in the desert with the cattle, he drank strong coffee with lots of _____ to stay awake at night.
2. The cowboys also sang music when they traveled to town to _____ and have a good time.
3. When they _____ their friends and families on holidays like _____, they usually sang and played country music.
4. _____ western music is very old.
5. They also added instruments from their homes, like _____, _____, and spoons.
6. Cowboys had to take care of the _____.
7. A cowboy's life was lonely and _____.

8. Sometimes they played ————————— guitars or harmonicas.
9. He also sang music to the cattle to ————————— them.
10. They did not run away if he sang beautiful, ————————— music.
11. Later they used ————————— and other instruments.

B Vocabulary (new context)

dangerous	bottles	caffeine	pieces
either	peaceful	cans	visit
alone	hotel	violin	calms
Thanksgiving	relaxes	cattle	country

1. Some people cannot sleep after they drink coffee. The ————————— keeps them awake.
2. It is ————————— to drive a car on icy roads.
3. You can buy vegetables and soup in —————————.
4. You can buy orange juice in cans and —————————.
5. People in the United States have a big dinner on ————————— because it is a very important family holiday.
6. Our children ————————— their grandparents every week.
7. When a war ends, the countries are —————————.
8. Some people live in the city and others live in the —————————.
9. ————————— are mammals.
10. Some people do not like to be —————————.
11. Mario wants to study ————————— the guitar or the
    —————————.
12. Sometimes classical music ————————— and ————————— people.

C Vocabulary Review

Underline the word that does not belong.

1. peace, soldier, army, war
2. motorcycle, truck, automobile, airplane
3. around, eastern, southern, western
4. guayule, tree, plastic, petroleum
5. violin, guitar, cassette, harmonica

6. cattle, fans, composers, performers
7. grass, caffeine, rice, palm
8. lovely, sweet, afraid, calm
9. listen, relax, express, slave

D Questions

1. Where did country western music come from?
*2. Why was a cowboy's life dangerous?
3. When did the cowboys sing?
4. What instruments do people use to play country western music?
*5. Where did many country people come from?
6. When country people visited their families on holidays, what did they do to have a good time?
7. What does country western music talk about?
8. Why do people all over the world like country western music?

E Comprehension: True/False/No Information

_____ 1. Many fans like to dance to country western music.
_____ 2. Country western music is new.
_____ 3. Country western music came from the American West and the American South.
_____ 4. The cattle became calm when they listened to the cowboy's songs.
_____ 5. Cowboys sometimes had to stay awake all night.
_____ 6. Cowboys always stayed alone in the desert.
_____ 7. Many country people came from Malaysia, China, and eastern Australia.
_____ 8. Country singers sing about unusual ideas.
_____ 9. Some fans enjoy country western music instead of rock and roll.

Latin Music and Salsa

LESSON

Pre-reading Questions

1. Did you ever hear a salsa band?
2. Can you play any of these instruments?
3. Do you like salsa?

Latin Music and Salsa

Latin music is very **common** in countries where people speak Spanish and Portuguese. However, now people all over the world can enjoy it. This music comes from Mexico, the
5 Caribbean, Central America, and South America. "Salsa" is one kind of Latin music. Big cities like Miami, New York, San Juan, Havana, or Panama City have their own kinds of salsa.

Latin music is a mixture of European
10 music and African music. It has a strong **beat.** Many years ago people played Latin music mostly on guitars with drums, but now whole **orchestras** with lots of other instruments play it. Latin music sounds very emotional.
15 Composers of Latin music express their feelings in their music. Sometimes they are very happy, and sometimes they are sad. Ruben Blades and Juan Luis Guerra are two famous modern Latin American composers. They perform their own
20 music with their own orchestras.

People can play Latin music and salsa at home or when they visit their friends. Sometimes salsa fans play **cards** in the afternoon or late at night on weekends or holidays
25 **while** they listen to Latin music. Some people bring guitars and play them while they sing. The other people relax and enjoy the music,

cards

when, at the same time

but they don't stop the card **game.** They **roast** or **bake** Latin food in the **<u>oven</u>** or **fry** it on top 30 of the stove in oil. When the food is ready, they stop playing cards. They listen to music while they eat. The food **tastes** good.

oven

People who dance enjoy Latin music because it is easy to dance to. The beat is very 35 strong and interesting. Dancers can move their whole bodies. They can dance alone or with someone. Other people enjoy listening to Latin music. Usually, the words are in Spanish or Portuguese, but sometimes they are in 40 English or other languages. Many Latin songs have beautiful words, but if a person does not understand them, it is not important. A person can still enjoy the music. The sound is **international.**

A Vocabulary

oven	beat	common	fry
international	cards	while	bake
orchestras	game	roast	tastes

1. Sometimes salsa fans play _____ in the afternoon or late at night on weekends or holidays _____ they listen to Latin music.
2. Latin music is very _____ in countries where people speak Spanish and Portuguese.
3. They _____ or _____ Latin food in the _____ or _____ it on top of the stove in oil.
4. The food _____ good.
5. It has a strong _____.
6. The sound is _____.
7. Many years ago people played Latin music mostly on guitars with drums, but now whole _____ with lots of other instruments play it.
8. The other people relax and enjoy the music, but they don't stop the card _____.

B Vocabulary (new context)

beat	common	cards	oven
baked	game	while	tastes
roast	international	fry	orchestra

1. Rita usually listens to music _____ she studies.
2. Carmen _____ a chocolate cake this morning.
3. Many people enjoy playing _____.
4. Who won the soccer _____?
5. Sometimes we _____ meat in oil on top of the stove. We bake or _____ food in the _____.
6. There is a dance tomorrow night for the _____ students. They are from different countries.
7. Rock and roll fans enjoy the _____ of the music.
8. Classical music is _____ all over the world.
9. Chocolate cake _____ better than grass.

C Vocabulary Review

express	boring	job	design
plan	relax	religion	Thanksgiving
museum	so	disease	energy
even	sections	skin	around

1. This television program is _____. Let's turn it off. It's not interesting.
2. What is your _____? Are you a Christian?
3. Most American students spend _____ with their families. It's an important holiday.
4. Music is a way to _____ emotion.
5. Some people love jazz. They _____ listen to it during breakfast.
6. Most people like to _____ after work or class.
7. There are _____ 200 students in the English program.
8. Do you _____ to go to the volleyball game tonight?
9. What kind of _____ do you want after you get your Master's degree?
10. The book has four _____. Each one is about a different subject.
11. There are some beautiful new photographs in the art _____.
12. Pictures of palm trees on a building make a beautiful _____.

D Questions

1. Where does Latin music come from?
2. What is "salsa"?
3. Name some cities that have their own types of salsa.
4. Latin music is a mixture of what kinds of music?
*5. Why does Latin music have a strong beat?
6. Who are Juan Luis Guerra and Ruben Blades?
*7. What are some things to do while you are listening to Latin music?
8. What is the difference between roasting and frying?
9. How does a person dance to Latin music?
*10. How is Latin music different from the blues or country western music?

E Comprehension: True/False

_____ 1. Caribbean countries have salsa.

_____ 2. Both African and European music helped make Latin music.

_____ 3. Ruben Blades usually performs with Juan Luis Guerra's orchestra.

_____ 4. Latin music does not express emotion.

_____ 5. Latin food tastes good.

_____ 6. It is difficult to dance to Latin music.

_____ 7. If you can't understand Spanish or Portuguese, you can't enjoy Latin music.

_____ 8. Salsa fans sometimes listen to Latin music while they play cards, cook, and eat.

_____ *9. If you want to dance to music, it's important to listen to the beat.

_____ 10. Many Latin songs have beautiful words.

F Main Idea and Supporting Details

Put the number of the supporting details after the topics. Some supporting details are about more than one topic.

a. Jazz _____   e. Blues _____

b. Country Music _____   f. Western Music _____

c. Rock and Roll _____   g. Latin Music _____

d. Classical Music _____ h. Salsa _____

1. It is common in countries where people speak Spanish.
2. It began during the 1950s.
3. Musicians play it differently each time.
4. Some of it does not show emotion.
5. San Juan, Havana, Miami, and Panama City have it.
6. Videos of its performers are very popular.
7. It is very emotional.
8. B. B. King plays it on "Lucille."
9. Bach, Haydn, and Mozart composed some of it.
10. People like to dance to it.
11. Cowboys sang this to the cattle.
12. People from Ireland, Scotland, and England sang this.
13. It came from the African slaves' music.
14. It talks about common ideas.
15. It expresses sad feelings, sometimes in a funny way.

Word Study

A Questions: Past Tense

be: Put **was** or **were** before the subject.

		subject	
Example:		**Tom**	**was** home last night.
	Was	**Tom**	home last night?

other verbs: Put **did** at the beginning of the sentence. Use the simple verb.

		subject	verb
Example:		**The farmers**	**planted** corn last spring.
	Did	**the farmers**	**plant** corn last spring?

Change these sentences to past tense questions.

1. The dancers listened to the music.
2. The orchestra ate dinner after the performance.
3. Their roast was in the oven for two hours.
4. Europeans and Africans fought wars with each other.
5. The cowboys raised cattle in the country.
6. The cook fried some thin pieces of meat.
7. The band sold compact discs to fans at the nightclub.
8. The blues singers were asleep on the bus.
9. Our neighbor went to San Francisco to hear Wynton Marsalis.

B Irregular Verbs

Memorize these irregular verbs. Put the right verb form in each blank.

Simple	Past	Simple	Past
do	did	go	went
get	got	give	gave
see	saw	sell	sold

(do)   1. Carlos _____ his homework early
            yesterday.

(get)   2. Did you _____ a good grade on your test?

(see)   3. Helen _____ her friends at the Student
            Union this morning at breakfast time.

(go)   4. They _____ to the football game last
            Saturday.

(give)   5. We _____ our mother a birthday present
            every year.

(sell)   6. Did the Browns _____ their house?

(be)   7. Paul and Robert _____ at home last night.

(grow)   8. Rubber _____ in Malaysia.

(think) 9. I _____ of the answer after the teacher
            asked someone else.

(take) 10. Will you _____ the TOEFL next month?

(eat)   11. We _____ pizza for lunch yesterday.

(come) 12. All the students _____ to the class party
            last night.

C -ly Adverbs

An adverb describes a verb. Many adverbs end in **-ly.** We can add
-ly to many adjectives.

> Example: slow – slowly

> Spelling: If the word ends in **y,** change the **y** to **i.**

>   easy – easily   day – daily

>   If the word ends in **-ble,** drop the **le.**

>   possible – possibly

**Add -*ly* to each adjective. Then use the correct adverb in the blanks.
Underline the verb.**

easy	different	cheap	busy
happy	day	possible	warm

1. You must dress _____ in winter or you will catch a
    cold.
2. You can _____ do the homework in a half hour. There
    are only three short exercises.
3. People from Spain and Mexico speak Spanish, but they speak a little

    _____ .
4. Could I _____ borrow your car? I need one this afternoon.
5. The English classes meet _____ .
6. You can live _____ if you live in a dormitory, cook
    your own food, and ride a bicycle.

D　Word Forms: Noun and Verb = Same

Many words have the same form for both the noun and the verb. Read these words. Then choose the right word for each sentence. Use the correct verb form, and singular or plural nouns.

Verb	Noun
feed	feed
use	use
poison	poison
plants	plant
taste	taste
cook	cook
work	work
drink	drink

1. Ruth has lovely _____ in front of her house. She _____ them last spring.
2. Robert is a good _____. He likes to bake cakes and he also _____ international dishes.
3. What are you eating? Can I have a _____? I never _____ that kind of food before.
4. Do you _____ coffee? Would you like a cold _____?
5. I have a lot of _____ to do. I _____ all day yesterday, but the _____ isn't finished.
6. Farmers buy one kind of _____ for chickens. They _____ their horses something different.

E　Writing

Write real information in your answers.

1. What kinds of music do you enjoy most? Why?
2. Choose two of the kinds of music in *Unit 4*. Tell how they are alike. Then tell how they are different.
3. Describe your country's national music or some other kind of music not in *Unit 4*.

Video Highlights

A Before You Watch

Walk around the class and ask questions. Write a classmate's name to the right of each description.

Example:

Q: Do you like to sing?

A: Yes, I do.

Find someone who...	Classmate's Name
...loves to sing.	*Gabriela*
...can play the guitar.	
...watches music videos.	
...likes country music.	
...likes to wear blue jeans.	
...doesn't like music at all.	
...can write songs.	

B As You Watch

What kind of music is the video about? Check only one.

©CNN

____ Jazz and Blues
____ Rock and Roll
____ Country Western
____ Classical
____ Latin and Salsa

C After You Watch

1. Which of these sentences are true about all three singers in the video?

   _____ They are all women.
   _____ They all write their own songs.
   _____ They all wear hats when they sing.
   _____ They all play the guitar.

2. Work with a partner or a small group of your classmates. Write in missing facts about each of the singers in the video. If you need to, watch the video again to find the answers.

   The name of Sherrie Austin's
   new album: _____

                                           _____

   The kind of clothes Michael
   Peterson likes to wear: _____

                                           _____

                                           _____

   What Matraca Berg
   wants to do now: _____

                                           _____

Activity Page

A Draw the Word

What instrument is missing from each of the pictures? Finish the picture by drawing in the missing instrument. Then write the name of the instrument next to the picture.

_____   _____   _____

B Music Bingo

Write one word from the list below in each box. When everyone is ready, your teacher will call out a vocabulary word. If you have written the word in a square, mark it with an **X.** Whoever has five **X**'s in a row, wins Bingo.

Vocabulary Words to Choose From

alone	add	beat	boring	blues	caffeine	calm
cards	common	composers	classical	dangerous	design	express
fans	feelings	game	harmonica	holiday	instrument	record
jazz	nervous	orchestra	popular	peaceful	performer	
soft	tastes	video	violins	visit	while	

Dictionary Page

Understanding Grammar

1. Look up each of the words below in your dictionary to find out if they are adjectives or nouns. Write *noun* or *adjective* next to each word. If the word you looked up is an adjective, change it to a noun and if it is a noun, change it to an adjective.

   Example:

   boring *adjective*   *boredom (noun)*

   a. classical _____   _____

   b. peaceful _____   _____

   c. danger _____   _____

   d. natural _____   _____

   e. nerve _____   _____

2. Use the correct forms of the words you identified above to complete these sentences.

   a. Gabriela doesn't like _____ music.

   b. After many years of war, the people prayed for _____.

   c. Some of the animals in the rain forest are _____ to humans.

   d. For thousands of years, the Bakas lived close to _____.

   e. The singer was _____ when she first walked on stage.

Occupations

Context Clues

1. Marie is **un**happy this week. Her parents didn't telephone her, and she failed a test.
   a. not
   b. in
   c. very
   d. a little

2. Fishing boats sometimes come back to the land if there is a **storm.**
   a. sunshine
   b. some fish
   c. bad weather
   d. good weather

3. When the sun goes down, it gets **dark.**
   a. thick
   b. not easy
   c. soft
   d. not light

4. At my apartment house, children can use the pool in the morning, and **adults** can use it in the afternoon.
   a. children
   b. teenagers
   c. men and women
   d. babies

5. The animal died because it ate something **toxic.**
   a. good
   b. poisonous
   c. sweet
   d. natural

6. I feel very cold. What is the **temperature?**
   a. How cold or hot is it?
   b. How far away is it?
   c. What time is it?
   d. Where is it?

7. Betty's baby was born with a **terrible** disease. He lived only a few hours.
   a. good
   b. bad
   c. very good
   d. very bad

8. Try to speak English **quickly.** Don't stop and think about every word.
   a. slowly
   b. poorly
   c. fast
   d. well

9. Alexander Graham Bell **invented** the telephone. There were no phones before that.
   a. made the first one
   b. called
   c. talked on
   d. sold

An Environmental Engineer

LESSON

1

Pre-reading Questions

1. What is the man doing? Why?

2. What is in the back of the picture?

3. Does your country have laws to keep the air and water clean?

An Environmental Engineer

Stephen Martinez is an **environmental engineer.** He works in many places, both inside and outside. He works for companies and for the government. Today he is looking for
5 dangerous gas and other **toxic substances.** Sometimes they have no taste or smell, but they can poison people, animals, or plants. He is testing the **dirt,** air, and water near a large **factory.** He is **digging** a **hole.** He is using
10 special **tools** to collect **samples.**

Many countries need environmental engineers. In the modern world, more governments are paying for a cleaner environment. They do not want factories to **pollute** the earth, air, or
15 water. They also want factories to store toxic substances in a safe way.

Now Stephen Martinez is **covering** the holes and finishing the tests. He is studying his mixtures and **laying** down his tools. He is
20 finished for the day. Now he can relax.

Today is a good day for the company. Stephen Martinez did not find any toxic substances. **Unlike** another factory yesterday, this factory is clean. It is not polluting the air,
25 water, or soil. It is safe for animals, plants, birds, and other living things.

toxic

factory

make unclean

digging a hole

un = not

sample

tools

A Vocabulary

unlike	toxic	dirt	hole
engineer	samples	collect	plan
substances	laying	environmental	digging
factory	pollute	covering	tools

1. Today he is looking for dangerous gas and other _____ _____.
2. Now Stephen Martinez is _____ the holes and finishing the tests.
3. _____ another factory yesterday, this factory is clean.
4. He is studying his mixtures and _____ down his tools.
5. Stephen Martinez is an _____ _____.
6. He is testing the _____, air, and water near a large _____.
7. He is using special _____ to collect _____.
8. He is _____ a _____.
9. They do not want factories to _____ the earth, air, or water.

B Vocabulary (new context)

unlike	toxic	dirty	hole
engineer	samples	mixture	bottles
substances	lay	environment	dig
factory	pollutes	cover	tools

1. Some farmers have to _____ a well to get water.
2. A mechanic uses _____ to fix cars.
3. Please _____ your books on the table.
4. Alan has to clean his apartment because it is very _____.
5. There is a _____ in my shoe. I have to buy a new pair.
6. _____ oranges, dates can grow in the desert.
7. _____ the pans when you cook. You will save energy.
8. Mohammed is studying at the university to become an _____.
9. Air, water, and soil are all part of our _____.

10. That _____ makes rubber tires.
11. Dirty water from rivers in big cities _____ the ocean.
12. _____ _____ make you sick if you eat or drink them.
13. Which of these two color _____ do you like better?

C Vocabulary Review

game	while	listen	cards
dangerous	caffeine	usually	strong
either	country	nearly	visit
alone	Thanksgiving	soon	soft

1. Are you going to the picnic _____ or with your friends?
2. Please sit down _____ you wait.
3. Ann is planning to visit _____ London or Paris next summer.
4. We live in the _____, far away from the city.
5. Does the _____ in coffee make you nervous?
6. My roommate has some free time and he is playing _____ with his friends. What card _____ are they playing?
7. A swimming pool can be a _____ place for small children.
8. It is _____ time to go. Hurry up!
9. Hate and love are _____ emotions.
10. Will your parents visit you _____ or will they be here next summer?

D Questions

1. What does an environmental engineer do?
2. What are toxic substances?
3. Why is Stephen Martinez digging a hole?
*4. Why do we need a clean environment?
5. How do some factories pollute the environment?
6. Can you taste or smell all toxic substances?
7. Why is Stephen Martinez laying down his tools?
8. Why is this factory safe for living things?

E Comprehension: Sequence

The sentences below tell you how Stephen Martinez, an environmental engineer, tests for pollution. Number the sentences in the right order. What does he do first? What does he do second and third? The first one is done for you.

_____ He digs a hole.
___1___ He goes to work.
_____ He covers the hole.
_____ He collects soil samples.
_____ He finishes the tests.
_____ He relaxes.
_____ He studies his mixtures.
_____ He lays down his tools.

F Main Idea

1. Many dangerous substances have no taste or smell.
2. Environmental engineers help make the environment safe.
3. Governments pay for environmental engineers.

A Human Resources Manager

LESSON

2

Pre-reading Questions

1. Where does this woman work?

2. Is she a worker or a boss?

3. What are some of the papers on her desk?

2

A Human Resources Manager

Wanda Cheung is a **human resources manager.** She works for a large company. Right now she is teaching a class. Her students are not children but **adults.** They are man-
5 agers. They are learning how to talk with the workers and how to help them. They are find-ing answers to the worker's questions.

Modern companies understand that workers are people. Happy people work better
10 and are more **productive** than unhappy workers. Wanda Cheung's job is to keep both the workers and the managers happy. Her job is also to **motivate** the workers. She is doing a good job. Her company is twenty percent
15 more productive now than it was before.

Now Wanda Cheung is sitting at her desk in her office. Many **applications** from people who want to be workers are **lying** on the desk. Letters from workers and managers also **reach**
20 her office.

It is the end of the day, and Wanda Cheung is tired. It is **dark** outside and a **storm** is coming. A worker from the office **below** Wanda's office is saying goodnight.

≠ children

application

dark ≠ light

storm = bad weather

under

A   Vocabulary

human	resources	storm	lying
dark	manager	below	productive
reach	applications	adults	motivate

1. Many _____ from people who want to be workers are _____ on her desk.
2. Her job is also to _____ the workers.
3. Her students are not children but _____.
4. A worker from the office _____ Wanda's office is saying good night.
5. It is _____ outside and a _____ is coming.
6. Wanda Cheung is a _____ _____ _____.
7. Letters from workers and managers also _____ her office.
8. Happy people work better and are more _____ than unhappy people.

B   Vocabulary (new context)

reach	manager	dark	daylight
adults	below	lying	application
humans	storm	motivates	productive

1. University students are not children. They are _____.
2. The people in the apartment _____ ours are very noisy.
3. If you want to attend the university, you have to send an _____.
4. The plane leaves at 3:00. It will _____ New York at 5:15.
5. There was a bad _____ last night. The wind blew down several trees.
6. Dan is swimming, and Tom is _____ beside the pool.
7. If a worker sleeps and eats well, she will be more _____.
8. People are _____, not animals.
9. After the sun sets, it gets _____ outside and the street lights come on.
10. The money they earn _____ many people to do a good job.

C Vocabulary Review

Match the words that mean the same.

Column A	Column B
1. unlike _____	a. usual
2. calm _____	b. not interesting
3. hard _____	c. different
4. boring _____	d. feeling
5. dig _____	e. dirt
6. common _____	f. put something over
7. dangerous _____	g. cook in the oven
8. cover _____	h. bottle
9. bake _____	i. or
10. emotion _____	j. difficult
11. either _____	k. make a hole
	l. peaceful
	m. not safe

D Questions

1. What does a human resources manager do?
2. Who sends applications to Wanda Cheung?
3. Who are Wanda Cheung's students?
4. What are Wanda Cheung's students learning?
5. What is the difference between happy workers and unhappy workers?
6. Who keeps both the workers and the managers happy?
7. How does the company know that Wanda Cheung is doing a good job?
8. Where are the letters and applications that reach Wanda Cheung?
*9. How do the workers feel about Wanda Cheung?

E Comprehension

1. Wanda Cheung's students are ———.
   a. engineers
   b. managers
   c. companies
   d. families

2. Wanda Cheung wants the ——— to be happy.
   a. workers
   b. managers
   c. children
   d. a and b

3. The company is ——— more productive now than it was before it had a human resources manager.
   a. 20 percent
   b. 30 percent
   c. 50 percent
   d. 10 percent

*4. The human resources manager has to ——— the workers.
   a. listen to
   b. understand
   c. motivate
   d. all of these

F Main Idea

1. Unhappy people work poorly.
2. Wanda Cheung teaches classes and works at her desk.
3. Human resources managers make companies better.

A Computer Information Specialist

LESSON

3

Pre-reading Questions

1. Do you know how to use a computer?

2. What is the man doing? What is the woman doing?

3. Where do we use computers?

A Computer Information Specialist

Katherine Boudreaux is a **computer** information **specialist.** Right now she is teaching a class about computers. She is teaching the workers how to change part of the computer.
5 The computer is **upside down,** so she is **holding on** to it.

In Ms. Boudreaux's class, the students are learning to relax. They feel afraid of the computers. Now, they have a computer beside
10 them. Some of them are very nervous.

In rooms with computers, the **temperature** has to be exactly right, not too high and not too **low.** No dirt **at all** can get into the computers. For example, one worker cannot use his computer now because he is eating a **sandwich.**
15

Computer information specialists do many different jobs. They have to **invent** ways for computers to help managers and workers in all parts of a company. They also tell their
20 company when to buy new computers and what kind to buy.

Efficient use of computers can make companies more productive. Computer information specialists try to make the whole
25 **system,** human and **electronic,** work efficiently.

upside down

low ≠ high   **holding on**

make the first one

temperature

sandwich

A Vocabulary

electronic	system	sandwich	at all
temperature	holding on	upside down	specialist
low	invent	computer	efficient

1. _____ use of computers can make companies more productive.
2. They have to _____ ways for computers to help managers and workers in all parts of a company.
3. Computer information specialists try to make the whole _____, human and _____, work efficiently.
4. The computer is _____, so she is _____ to it.
5. No dirt _____ can get into the computers.
6. For example, one worker cannot use his computer now because he is eating a _____.
7. In rooms with computers, the _____ has to be exactly right, not too high and not too _____.
8. Katherine Boudreaux is a _____ information _____.

B Vocabulary (new context)

temperature	efficient	specialist	electronics
system	hold on	at all	low
computer	invented	sandwich	upside down

1. The water _____ on that farm is very good.
2. Elena is studying _____ at the university.
3. Most governments are not very _____.
4. If you can't find a seat in the bus, you have to stand up. You also have to _____ to something.
5. A hearing-impaired person sometimes cannot hear anything _____.
6. The _____ is high today. It is 40 degrees C.
7. We don't have time for a big dinner, so please eat a _____.

8. Please turn your paper around. I can't read it _____.
9. My doctor is a _____. He only takes care of ears.
10. Scientists _____ a new way to make rubber.
11. Some students get high grades. Others get _____ grades.

C Vocabulary Review

saving	compose	emotion	bottles
bad for	performers	cans	stars
listen to	compact discs	relax	tastes
orchestra	canned	strong	cassettes

1. _____ food has salt in it.
2. Martha is _____ money for her summer vacation.
3. Do you like to _____ classical music?
4. Love is a strong _____.
5. Some rock _____ earn millions of dollars.
6. Most soft drinks come in _____ and cans.
7. The sky is beautiful tonight. We can see hundreds of _____.
8. Too much sugar and salt are _____ the body.
9. How _____ are you? Can you pick up an elephant?
10. Many students study English by listening to _____.
11. This fish _____ bad. Did it come from polluted water?

D Questions

1. Who is learning to use computers?
*2. Is it a good idea to use a computer while you are eating? Why or why not?
3. How is the temperature in the computer room?
4. Why is Ms. Boudreaux holding on to the computer?
5. Why are some of the students nervous?
*6. Can a computer find information faster or slower than a human can?
*7. Name some places that need computers.
8. What does a computer information specialist do?

E Comprehension: True/False

_____ 1. Katherine Boudreaux is teaching workers how to eat a sandwich.
_____ 2. Computers have to be very clean.
_____ 3. A computer works well in a very hot room.
_____ 4. A computer specialist can change parts of a computer.
_____ 5. Some students are afraid of computers.
_____ 6. Workers can learn to relax with computers.
_____ 7. Computers can help both managers and workers.
_____ 8. Companies can be more productive if they have good computer systems.
_____ 9. Computers are electronic.

F Main Idea

1. Computer information specialists help companies use computers better.
2. It is important for all students to learn to use computers.
3. All workers need computers.

A Firefighter

LESSON

4

Pre-reading Questions

1. What is the woman doing?

2. What other things does she do in her job?

3. Is her job dangerous or safe?

A Firefighter

Glenda Smith is a **firefighter.** Right now, she and many other firefighters are going to a **terrible** fire at a factory. The people at the factory are afraid. They want the firefighters to **appear** soon to **put out** the fire. The fire is very hot. It smells bad, and people cannot breathe.

very bad

The firefighters are at the factory now. They are having some **problems** with the fire. There are rubber tires, fertilizer, tanks of gas, and other toxic substances **nearby.** These substances are very dangerous when they burn. They can pollute the air in the whole **area.**

near

Glenda Smith attended school to be a firefighter. She learned about dangerous substances. She knows how to help people breathe during a fire and how to carry large people. She can run and **jump** in difficult conditions.

Now Glenda and the other firefighters are coming back to the fire **station.** They feel happy. They **solved** the problems and put out the fire **quickly.** No one was hurt. They put out the fire efficiently with the help of a computer in the fire truck.

fast

A group of children is **passing** through the fire station to learn about fighting fires. Glenda is showing them how she cleans her truck and her tools. She is telling them how much she likes her work.

When the fire station is quiet, Glenda and the other firefighters can relax. They can eat, sleep, listen to music, and play cards. **Suddenly,** they hear a loud sound. It is the fire **alarm.** They are going to fight another fire.

30

35

pass = move, go

A Vocabulary

station	firefighter	terrible	jump
quickly	solved	alone	nearby
alarm	problems	put out	millions
area	appear	suddenly	passing

1. They want the firefighters to _____ soon to _____ the fire.

2. They _____ the problems and put out the fire _____.

3. There are rubber tires, fertilizer, tanks of gas, and other toxic substances _____.

4. _____, they hear a loud sound.

5. It is the fire _____.

6. Glenda Smith is a _____.

7. They are having some _____ with the fire.

8. Right now, she and many other firefighters are going to a _____ fire at a factory.

9. She can run and _____ in difficult conditions.

10. A group of children is _____ through the fire station to learn about fighting fires.

11. Now Glenda and the other firefighters are coming back to the fire _____.

12. They can pollute the air in the whole _____.

B Vocabulary (new context)

nearby	alone	appeared	suddenly
terrible	quickly	jumped	problem
passed	solve	areas	station
put out	alarm	loud	firefighters

1. Can you _____ this math problem? 763 x 44 = ?
2. Wars are _____. They kill thousands of people.
3. I waited thirty minutes for Isamu and then he _____. He was sorry that he was late.
4. Ms. Johnson's children all got good grades and _____ to the next grade.
5. Water hyacinths grow in tropical _____.
6. Ted _____ through the air to catch the ball.
7. You have to think _____ when you are taking a test.
8. Liz lives on Peach Street, and Jean lives _____.
9. Water hyacinths are a _____ in some countries.
10. Peter is waiting for the bus at the bus _____.
11. When you are asleep and hear the _____ in the morning, turn it off and get up.

C Vocabulary Review

Match the words that mean the opposite.

Column A
1. dark _____
2. soft _____
3. below _____
4. near _____
5. child _____
6. interesting _____
7. common _____
8. natural _____
9. cover _____
10. cool _____

Column B
a. ground
b. boring
c. loud
d. unnatural
e. above
f. warm
g. unusual
h. adult
i. uncover
j. light
k. far

D Questions

1. What nearby substances are very dangerous when they burn?
2. What can pollute the air in the whole area?
3. Where is the fire?
4. Name three things Glenda Smith learned at firefighter school.
5. What helped the firefighters put out the fire efficiently?
6. Why are the children passing through the fire station?
7. How do Glenda and the other firefighters relax?
*8. Why do they need to relax?

E Comprehension

1. _____ are very dangerous when they burn.
   a. fertilizers
   b. tanks of gas
   c. rubber tires
   d. all of these

2. Firefighters _____ fires.
   a. put out
   b. start
   c. enjoy
   d. poison

3. Fires _____.
   a. smell good
   b. are afraid
   c. pollute the area
   d. cannot breathe

4. To be a firefighter, Glenda Smith _____.
   a. attended classes
   b. took tests
   c. studied hard
   d. a, b, and c

5. In the fire truck there is a _____.
   a. game of cards
   b. fire
   c. computer
   d. plan

6. Fighting fires is a _____ job.
   a. dirty
   b. safe
   c. boring
   d. a and c

F Main Idea

1. Fires are dangerous.
2. A firefighter's job has many different parts.
3. Some women are firefighters.

A Chimney Sweep

LESSON

5

Pre-reading Questions

1. Is this man wearing work clothes?
2. What is he going to do inside the house?
3. Do you know anyone who dresses like this?

5

A Chimney Sweep

Bruce Chapman is a **chimney** sweep. He is going to work. His clothes are unusual for a worker. He is wearing a tall hat, a formal coat, and a **silk** tie. He has a broom in his hand.

5 Many chimney sweeps dress this special way. Now Bruce is ringing the **bell**. After he **enters** the house, he changes his clothes.

Sweeping chimneys is a very old and dangerous job. Chimney sweeps today use

10 expensive, modern **equipment** instead of brooms. They only carry the brooms. They store their equipment in their trucks.

Bruce has air tanks so he does not breathe toxic substances. Now he is covering his body,

15 face, and hands to clean the chimney. Bruce has tools of many different **shapes**. He is **filling** the room with his tools.

Bruce finds **spider webs,** insects, and a small dead animal in the chimney. Now the

20 chimney is clean, but Bruce's work is not finished **yet.** He is cleaning the room and putting his tools back into the truck.

Chimney sweeps save lives. Chimney fires are dangerous and expensive. Twenty-eight

25 percent of all house fires start in unsafe, dirty chimneys. If people do not have **enough** money to pay a chimney sweep, they clean their own chimneys.

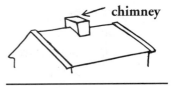

chimney

goes in

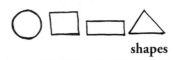

bells

shapes

spider

web

A Vocabulary

spider	sweep	filling	chimney
enters	enough	yet	webs
silk	bell	equipment	shapes

1. He is wearing a tall hat, a formal coat, and a _____ tie.
2. Now Bruce is ringing the _____.
3. He is _____ the room with his tools.
4. After he _____ the house, he changes his clothes.
5. Chimney sweeps today use expensive, modern _____ instead of brooms.
6. If people do not have _____ money to pay a chimney sweep, they clean their own chimneys.
7. Bruce Chapman is a _____ _____.
8. Bruce finds _____ _____, insects, and a small dead animal in the chimney.
9. Bruce has tools with many different _____.
10. Now the chimney is clean, but Bruce's work is not finished _____.

B Vocabulary (new context)

bell	spiders	enter	shape
enough	equipment	sweep	silk
chimney	fill	web	yet

1. It is summer, so we are going to _____ the swimming pool with water.
2. You can _____ the building through either the front or the side door.
3. Some people are afraid of _____, but most of them are not dangerous.
4. A circle is one _____. A square is another.
5. The _____ rings every hour on the hour. Then it is time for the classes to begin.
6. A spider catches insects in its _____.
7. Are you finished with my dictionary? No, not _____.

8. Leila has a beautiful new _____ dress.
9. When you clean your room, do not forget to _____ the floor.
10. Firefighters use a lot of _____.
11. If a plant does not get _____ water, it will die.
12. Most houses in tropical areas do not have a _____.

C   Vocabulary Review

dirty	tool	manager	reach
bake	lying	application	humans
temperature	strong	lower	invented
efficient	specialist	at all	rock

1. What is the _____ in the winter in your country? Is it cold?
2. Workers are _____, not animals.
3. Tony put all his _____ clothes in the washer, added some soap, and turned it on.
4. Ali is _____. He does his homework fast and correctly.
5. The _____ told the worker to take a vacation.
6. Children's school desks are _____ than adults' desks.
7. _____ music is popular with young people.
8. Keiko is _____ on the sofa. She is very tired.
9. Scientists _____ a new electronic tool.
10. To _____ Cape Verde, you travel west off the coast of Africa.
11. I have no money _____ with me. I forgot to bring any.
12. A mechanic uses one kind of _____. A carpenter uses a different kind because he works with wood.

D   Questions

1. Describe a chimney sweep.
*2. Why are his clothes unusual for a worker?
3. Is sweeping chimneys a new job?
4. What is one difference between chimney sweeps in the old days and modern chimney sweeps?

5. Does Bruce work in the same clothes he travels in? If not, how are his real work clothes different?
6. What things does Bruce find in the chimney?
7. What is Bruce doing after cleaning the chimney?
8. If a chimney gets very dirty, what can happen?
9. What do people do if they cannot pay for a chimney sweep?

E Comprehension: True/False/No Information

———— 1. Chimney sweeps study chimneys in a school.
———— 2. Bruce keeps his equipment in his truck.
———— *3. Wood fires can pollute the environment.
———— 4. Bruce's work is finished when the chimney is clean.
———— 5. Dirty chimneys are unsafe.
———— 6. Seventy-two percent of all house fires start in the kitchen.

F Main Idea

1. Chimney sweeps have an unusual job.
2. Modern jobs are different from jobs in the past.
3. Toxic substances come from fires.

Word Study

A Present Continuous Tense

Use the present continuous tense for something that is happening right now. Use **am, is,** or **are** and the **-ing** form of the verb (**be + v-ing**).

Example: Now she **is shopping** for food.
The birds **are flying** toward the south.

Spelling: 1. Use the **1-1-1** rule.
shop – shopping   put – putting

2. If the verb ends in **e,** drop the **e** and add **-ing.**
live – living   leave – leaving

3. If the verb ends in **ie,** change the **ie** to **y.**
lie – lying   die – dying

4. If the verb ends in **y,** don't make any changes.
study – studying   fly – flying

Write sentences in the present continuous tense. Tell something that is happening now. Use these verbs.

1. dig
2. jump
3. sit
4. work
5. plan

6. study
7. lie
8. fry
9. use
10. carry

B Irregular Verbs

1. Memorize these verb forms. Then use the past tense of each verb in a sentence.

	Simple	Past			Simple	Past
a.	become	became		e.	feel	felt
b.	buy	bought		f.	find	found
c.	fight	fought		g.	put	put
d.	bring	brought		h.	cut	cut

2. Write the past tense of these verbs:

a. see _____   h. sell _____
b. go _____   i. get _____
c. be _____   j. come _____
d. give _____   k. grow _____
e. make _____   l. teach _____
f. eat _____   m. take _____
g. think _____

C   Un-

Un- means **not.**

Add *un-* to each of these words. Then put the words in the blanks.

happy   popular   like   cover
hurt   afraid   kind   common

1. A water spider is _____. It lives only in Europe and parts of Asia.
2. Sam is often _____ to people so he is _____. People don't like him because he is not nice to them.
3. Carol is only twelve years old. She was alone in the house during a storm and she was _____.
4. The baby fell off a chair but she was _____.

D   Compound Words

Put a word from Column A with a word from Column B and make a compound word. Write it in Column C.

Column A	Column B	Column C
1. under	a. light	_____
2. near	b. mate	_____
3. sun	c. work	_____
4. sun	d. water	_____
5. spring	e. food	_____
6. under	f. not	_____
7. room	g. by	_____

Column A	Column B	Column C
8. sea	h. time	_____
9. home	i. line	_____
10. can	j. rise	_____

E Writing

Write real information in your answers.

1. Which one of the jobs in *Unit 5* is the most interesting to you? Why?
2. In your country, which of the five people in *Unit 5* could find a job most easily? Why?
3. In your country, which of the five people in *Unit 5* could not find a job easily? Why?

Video Highlights

Before You Watch

1. Interview a partner. Write your partner's answer below each question.
   a. What is your job now?

   _____

   b. Do you like your job? Why or why not?

   _____

   c. Is your job dangerous or safe? Explain.

   _____

   Report your partner's answers to the class.

2. Discuss this scene from the video with your classmates:

©CNN

What is happening?
Why do you think this firefighter likes his job?
What are some of the difficult things about a firefighter's job?

B As You Watch

Listen for these facts from the video. Write in the missing information.

The name of the firehouse	*Firehouse 11*
The number of firefighters on the crew.	
The number of fires and rescues each year.	

C After You Watch

1. Check the answers that fit with the question below.

   Why do these firefighters like their job?

It is exciting and full of action. ✓

There is never anything to do. _____

The firefighters like to save lives. _____

The part of Los Angeles they work in is peaceful and safe. _____

2. Complete this sentence, then share it with your classmates. I (want / do not want) to be a firefighter in Los Angeles, California because

_____.

Activity Page

Workplace Ladder

Play this game with 3–4 people. Choose one of your group to be the "judge." You will each need a coin or a button, and the group will need one die. All players begin with their coins (or buttons) on START.

coin

Follow these directions:
1. Put your coin (or button) on START.
2. Roll the die. Move your coin the same number of squares as the number on the die.
3. On each square, say the missing word and spell it correctly. The "judge" decides if you are right or wrong. If you are right, you get another turn. If you are wrong, it is the next player's turn.
4. The player who reaches FINISH first wins the game.

button

die

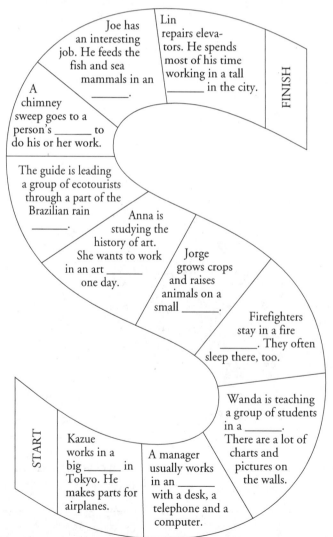

Joe has an interesting job. He feeds the fish and sea mammals in an _____.

Lin repairs elevators. He spends most of his time working in a tall _____ in the city.

FINISH

A chimney sweep goes to a person's _____ to do his or her work.

The guide is leading a group of ecotourists through a part of the Brazilian rain _____.

Anna is studying the history of art. She wants to work in an art _____ one day.

Jorge grows crops and raises animals on a small _____.

Firefighters stay in a fire _____. They often sleep there, too.

Wanda is teaching a group of students in a _____. There are a lot of charts and pictures on the walls.

START

Kazue works in a big _____ in Tokyo. He makes parts for airplanes.

A manager usually works in an _____ with a desk, a telephone and a computer.

176

Dictionary Page

Understanding Definitions

1. Write in the names of the people who do these things. Use your dictionary to check for meaning and spelling.

    Example: a person who fights fires: _a firefighter_ _____

    a. a person who manages workers: _____
    b. a person who protects the _____
       environment:
    c. a person who sweeps chimneys: _____
    d. a person who helps managers _____
       use computers:

2. Which of the following are people? Which are pieces of equipment? Complete the sentences with words from the list. Check your dictionary if you are not sure.

chimney sweep	screwdriver
hose	specialist
broom	computer
engineer	manager

    Example: A _scientist_ is a person.

    1. A(n) _____ is a person.
    2. A(n) _____ is a person.
    3. A(n) _____ is a person.
    4. A(n) _____ is a piece of equipment.
    5. A(n) _____ is a piece of equipment.
    6. A(n) _____ is a piece of equipment.
    7. A(n) _____ is a piece of equipment.

Interesting People of the World

Context Clues

1. Keiko has $100. Betty has $75. Betty has **less** money than Keiko.
   a. more
   b. the same as
   c. not as much as
   d. a lot of

2. There are hundreds of square kilometers of **forest** in the Amazon River area. There are trees everywhere.
   a. lots of trees
   b. some trees
   c. lots of water
   d. some water

3. The Browns are planning to **take a trip** to Florida this summer.
   a. fall down
   b. travel
   c. buy something
   d. give something

4. Beginning students know only **a few** English words. Advanced students know a lot.
   a. not very many
   b. quickly
   c. many
   d. alone

5. Children start to **attend** school when they are five or six years old.
   a. finish
   b. solve
   c. go to
   d. hold on

6. Eskimos **hunt** the polar bear. When they find one, they kill it.
   a. look for
   b. study
   c. hurt
   d. appear

7. What is your **age**? Are you twenty years old yet?
   a. How tall are you?
   b. Where are you from?
   c. How much do you weigh?
   d. How old are you?

8. **Perhaps** there will be large guayule farms some day.
   a. over
   b. maybe
   c. below
   d. at all

9. I was in California for a year but I did **not ever** visit San Diego. I was too busy to go there.
   a. never
   b. possibly
   c. probably
   d. suddenly

10. We must **somehow** stop using so much energy or we will use all of our petroleum.
    a. somebody
    b. in some place
    c. nobody
    d. in some way

11. When did you **arrive** at this university? Did you come here in September?
    a. come
    b. alone
    c. leave
    d. hold on

12. Kenya was a British **colony.** Mexico was a Spanish **colony.** Algeria was a French **colony.**
    a. a large coffee farm
    b. an international company
    c. a farming area
    d. a place or country that belongs to another country

13. Rio de Janeiro is on the east **coast** of Brazil.
    a. land with water around it
    b. mountain
    c. land near the sea
    d. lake

14. Java is the name of one **island** in Indonesia.
    a. water with land all around it
    b. land with water all around it
    c. country
    d. mountains

The Sami of Northern Europe

LESSON

Pre-reading Questions

1. How is the weather where these people live?

2. What kind of animal is in the picture?

3. Do these people travel in cars?

1

The Sami of Northern Europe

The Sami live in northern Norway, Sweden, Finland, and Russia. There are only about thirty-two thousand (32,000) of them, and most of them live a modern life on the
5 **coast** or in the **forests.** Only a few of them live a **traditional** life. These few mountain Sami are called **nomads** because they move from one place to another with their **reindeer.** Their life is almost the same as it was a thousand
10 years ago.

In winter the reindeer dig through the snow to find plants for their food. In spring these plants become very dry, and there are lots of insects. Then the Sami move their reindeer
15 to the coast. The deer live on the thick grass there until winter. When the snow becomes **deep,** the Sami and their reindeer begin moving slowly back to their winter homes. There is **less** snow there.
20 These nomads live in **tents** because they move so often. They make shoes, jackets, and pants of reindeer skin. They also wear beautiful blue and red traditional clothes. They walk or travel on **skis.** They have **sleds** too. Reindeer
25 pull the sleds.

coast = land by the sea/forest = area with lots of trees

skis

not as much

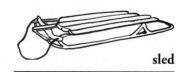

sled

The long **trips,** often in stormy weather, make life very hard for these nomads. More and more people are staying in villages on the coast. Sometimes a mother and her children

30 travel by car and meet the father in their winter home.

There will probably be no more Sami nomads in the **future.** People want a more **comfortable** life. However, the Sami will prob-

35 ably always wear their traditional clothes on holidays. They will teach their children the old stories and songs. People do not want to forget their traditions.

A Vocabulary

traditional	coast	trips	comfortable
clothes	forests	deep	skis
few	reindeer	blue	tents
future	sleds	nomads	less

1. Only a few of them live a _____ life.
2. There will probably be no more Sami nomads in the

   _____.

3. When the snow becomes _____, the Sami and their reindeer begin moving slowly back to their winter homes.
4. There are only about 32,000 of them, and most of them live a modern life on the _____ or in the _____.
5. People want a more _____ life.
6. These few mountain Sami are _____ because they move from one place to another with their _____.
7. The long _____, often in stormy weather, make life very hard for these nomads.
8. They have _____ too.
9. They walk or travel on _____.
10. There is _____ snow there.
11. These nomads live in _____ because they move so often.

B Vocabulary (new context)

forests	trip	traditional	stormy
tent	future	few	ski
nomads	slowly	comfortable	sleds
coast	deep	stories	less

1. Janet and Tom are going to take a _____ to England next year.
2. Eastern Canada has large _____. There are millions of trees.
3. The water in the Pacific Ocean is very _____.
4. In northern countries, children like to play on their _____ in winter. They also like to _____.
5. The Baker family likes to go camping. They sleep in a _____.
6. _____ in the Sahara Desert travel with their camels.
7. What are your plans for the _____? What are you going to do?
8. Most people in Saudi Arabia dress in _____ clothes. A few people wear western clothes.
9. This chair is not very _____. It is too hard.
10. Twelve is _____ than fifteen.
11. People who live on the _____ often eat a lot of fish.

C Vocabulary Review

Match the words that mean the same.

Column A

1. pass _____
2. terrible _____
3. below _____
4. alone _____
5. storm _____
6. over _____
7. quickly _____
8. web _____
9. adult _____
10. coast _____

Column B

a. fill
b. go or move
c. land near the sea
d. under
e. shape
f. very bad
g. with no light
h. not with anyone
i. above
j. a spider's home
k. man or woman
l. fast
m. bad weather

D Questions

1. In what countries do the Sami live?
2. Do they all move from one place to another?
3. What are nomads?
4. Does the life of Sami nomads change very much?
5. How do reindeer find their food in winter?
6. Why do these Sami move away from the coast in winter?
7. Why do they live in tents?
8. How do they travel?
9. What makes life hard for these nomads?
10. Why will these Sami probably change their lives?
*11. Where do other nomads live?
12. Why will the Sami teach their children the old songs and stories?
*13. Why do people want to keep their traditions?
*14. Are there roads in northern Scandinavia?

■E■ Comprehension: True/False

_____ 1. There are Sami in Russia.

_____ 2. Only a few Sami are nomads.

_____ 3. Sami nomads raise sheep.

_____ 4. Most Sami live in large cities.

_____ 5. Reindeer find their food on trees.

_____ 6. Sami nomads spend the summer on the coast.

_____ *7. Sami nomads probably eat reindeer meat.

_____ *8. They carry their tents on sleds.

_____ 9. Traveling in stormy weather is difficult.

_____ *10. Nomads in other countries probably want to keep their traditions and have a comfortable life too.

■F■ Main Idea

1. A few Sami live a traditional life but that life is difficult.
2. Sami nomads move their reindeer every summer and winter.
3. Sami want to keep some of their traditions.

The Ainu of Japan

LESSON

Pre-reading Questions

1. Where do these people live?

2. What do they look like?

3. Is their country warm or cold?

The Ainu of Japan

The Ainu live in northern Japan on the
island of Hokkaido. They do not look like
other Japanese. They have round, dark brown
eyes and **wavy** hair. Their skin is not dark but
5 **light.** The men have **beards** and **mustaches.**
Where did these people come from? Did they
come from Europe **across** Russia to Japan? Did
they come from Indonesia? Are they
completely different from all the other people
10 in the world? Nobody knows the answer to
these questions.

The Ainu were in Japan seven thousand
(7,000) years ago. In modern times, the
Japanese brought new diseases to Ainu villages.
15 Many people died. Today there are only a small
number of Ainu **left.** There are also about
25,000 people who are part Ainu.

The Ainu eat seafood and grow rice and
vegetables on their farms. The men **hunt** for
20 brown bears in the forests. They eat the meat
and sell the skins. The bear is also important in
their religion.

People make their houses from a kind of
grass. There is only one room inside. It has a
25 dirt floor with an open fire in the **middle.**
Their religion tells them that the house must
have one window on the east side.

land with water all around it

light ≠ dark

100%

 curly hair

 straight hair

 wavy hair

mustache

beard

Young Ainu **attend** school with other
Japanese. They speak Japanese, and many of
30 them don't know their own language. They
want to be like other young Japanese.

go to

The Sami in northern Europe want to **continue** their traditions. Some young Ainu don't
want to learn their traditions. When the older peo-
35 ple die, many Ainu traditions will die with them.

A Vocabulary

island	completely	middle	continue
attend	mustaches	wavy	light
across	beards	hunt	left

1. Did they come from Europe _____ Russia to Japan?
2. Today there are only a small number of Ainu _____.
3. Young Ainu _____ school with other Japanese.
4. The men have _____ and _____.
5. The men _____ for brown bears in the forests.
6. They have round, dark brown eyes and _____ hair.
7. It has a dirt floor with an open fire in the _____.
8. Are they _____ different from all the other people in the world?
9. The Sami in northern Europe want to _____ their traditions.
10. The Ainu live in northern Japan on the _____ of Hokkaido.
11. Their skin is not dark but _____.

B Vocabulary (new context)

continue	attend	mustache	light
wavy	middle	completely	beard
island	across	hunting	left

1. We ate all the bananas. There aren't any _____.
2. The students _____ finished the book. They did every page.
3. Number 5 is in the _____ of this exercise.

4. Carlos has _____ brown hair. He has a
   _____ and a _____, too.
5. Where did you _____ high school?
6. _____ is a popular sport in some countries.
7. Sarah walked _____ the street to the bank.
8. We did not have time to finish the lesson. We will _____
   it tomorrow.
9. We went to a beautiful _____ for our holiday.
10. Do not go out in the sun. Your skin is too _____.

C Vocabulary Review

hold on	upside down	suddenly	enough
appeared	area	solve	yet
silk	entered	bells	mixture
roast	invented	ears	hole

1. The number 6 is like a 9, but it is _____.
2. Water in a river cannot move when it is covered with water hyacinths.
   Scientists are trying to _____ this problem.
3. Superman suddenly _____ from the sky.
4. Thomas Edison _____ the electric light.
5. The manager worked sixteen hours yesterday. He does not have
   _____ energy to move fast today.
6. Fertilizer is a _____ of plant and animal substances.
7. Oscar _____ the class a week late.
8. Many Americans have _____ beef for Sunday dinner.
9. Some church _____ sound beautiful.
10. The engineer dug a _____ in the dirt.
11. Little children _____ to their mothers' hands when they
    walk across the street.
12. Did your cousin pass the TOEFL test _____?

D Questions

1. Where do the Ainu live?
2. What do they look like?
3. Where did they come from?
4. How many Ainu are there today?

*5. What will happen to the Ainu people if most of the children marry other Japanese?

6. Why do Ainu men hunt brown bears?

7. Describe a traditional Ainu house.

8. What language do young Ainu speak?

*9. Why do young Ainu want to be like other Japanese?

10. What will happen to Ainu traditions if the young people don't learn them?

E Comprehension

1. Ainu have _____ eyes.
   a. green
   b. black
   c. blue
   d. brown

2. Ainu are different from other Japanese because _____.
   a. they have hair
   b. they have eyes
   c. they have large hands
   d. they have round eyes

3. Today there are only _____ Ainu left.
   a. 300
   b. a small number of
   c. 15,000
   d. a large number of

*4. Ainu and other Japanese are alike because _____.
   a. they have grass houses
   b. they have wavy hair
   c. they hunt bears
   d. they eat seafood and rice

5. The Ainu house has a window on the east side _____.
   a. to let in sunlight
   b. because of their religion
   c. to look at the mountains
   d. to look for bears

6. Some young Ainu speak _____.
   a. only Ainu
   b. only Japanese
   c. Ainu and Japanese
   d. English

7. Young Ainu attend _____.
   a. Ainu schools
   b. Japanese dances
   c. Japanese schools
   d. soccer games

F Main Idea

Put the letter of the supporting details under the correct main ideas. Two of the details do not belong under a main idea.

1. **How an Ainu looks**　　2. **An Ainu's house**　　3. **Young Ainu**

a. The men have mustaches.
b. Many young Ainu speak only Japanese.
c. They want to be like other Japanese.
d. There is an open fire in the middle.
e. They were in Japan 7,000 years ago.
f. They have round eyes.
g. There is a dirt floor.
h. They attend Japanese schools.
i. They have wavy hair.
j. It is made of a kind of grass.
k. It has a window on the east side.
l. The men have beards.
m. They have light skin.

The Yanomami of the Amazon

LESSON

Pre-reading Questions

1. Do these people live in a warm or a cold climate?

2. Are they going to visit their friends?

3. Do these people need guns?

The Yanomami of the Amazon

The Yanomami people live in the Amazon forest between Venezuela and Brazil. They live in the tropical forest far away from other people. There are about 20,000 of them in 200
5 villages. Before scientists visited them, they knew nothing about other people in South America, about the government, or about modern life. They did not know they lived in Brazil or Venezuela. They lived in their own world.

10 The Yanomami were Stone **Age** people. They used stone tools. They had stone **axes** for cutting. They used **bamboo** knives. They ate bananas and palm fruit and hunted animals. Sometimes they ate **frogs** and insects. They
15 wore a few leaves for clothes.

Then government **officials** and scientists started to visit them often. They were studying the Yanomami for an unusual reason. The Yanomami are some of the most **violent** people
20 on earth. They kill each other often. They get angry quickly and stay angry for years. They **hit** their enemies with long **sticks.** Their villages are usually at war. Scientists want to know why humans make war. Other groups of people
25 live together and do not make war. Why are the yanomami so violent?

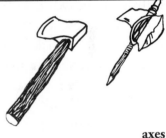

axes

time period

important government workers

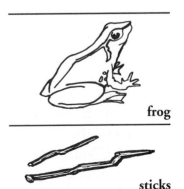

frog

sticks

30   Now the lives of the Yanomami are changing very fast. Visitors from the modern world are teaching them to eat different kinds of food with salt and fat. This food makes the Yanomami sick. It is bad for them. Now they make war on other villages with **metal** knives and guns. They have **cloth** now. Every time they get something new, they want more modern things. However, the modern things

35   are killing the yanomami. New diseases are killing them. Modern companies **mined** for gold. They cut down trees in the forest for wood. They also killed Yanomami. In 1991

40   Brazil and Venezuela made the Yanomami land into a park. No one can mine for gold or cut trees on this land. The governments want to save the Yanomami.

    The Yanomami are learning many new

45   things from the rest of the world. If we study them, we can learn something, too. **Perhaps** we   maybe have something more important to learn than to teach.

▣ Vocabulary

frogs	officials	sticks	perhaps
cloth	hit	violent	mining
bamboo	axes	metal	Age

1. _____ we have something more important to learn than to teach.
2. They _____ their enemies with long _____.
3. Then government _____ and scientists started to visit them often.
4. The Yanomami were Stone _____ people.
5. Sometimes they ate _____ and insects.
6. The Yanomami are some of the most _____ people on earth.

7. They make war on other villages with _____ knives and guns.
8. They have _____ now.
9. They had stone _____ for cutting.
10. They used _____ knives.
11. Modern companies _____ for gold.

■ B Vocabulary (new context)

age	violent	perhaps	metal
official	sticks	frog	axe
cloth	mining	hit	bamboo

1. People make clothes out of _____.
2. Stay away from Eduardo. He is a very _____ person.
3. A _____ lives in the water, but it cannot breathe under water.
4. When were you born? What is your _____?
5. Hiroshi isn't in class today. _____ he is sick.
6. Nadia's father is a government _____. He works in Washington.
7. Some desks are wooden. Some are _____.
8. Some people build a fire out of small _____.
9. The baseball player _____ the ball and ran around the bases.
10. Oscar cut down a tree with an _____.
11. _____ grows in a hot climate.

C   Vocabulary Review

Match the words that mean the opposite.

Column A

1. higher _____
2. cleaner _____
3. child _____
4. began _____
5. over _____
6. wet _____
7. upside down _____
8. more _____
9. future _____
10. alone _____
11. a few _____
12. terrible _____

Column B

a. right side up
b. across
c. a lot
d. lower
e. stopped
f. together
g. wonderful
h. under
i. middle
j. past
k. dirtier
l. less
m. adult
n. dry

D   Questions

1. Where do the Yanomami live?
2. How many Yanomami villages are there?
*3. What are Stone Age people?
*4. Why didn't the Yanomami know about other people?
5. Describe their tools.
6. What did they eat?
7. How are the Yanomami different from many other people on earth?
8. Why are scientists studying the Yanomami?
9. Name some changes in their lives.
10. What is killing the Yanomami?
11. What did Brazil and Venezuela do for the Yanomami?
*12. What can we learn from the Yanomami?
*13. What do you think will happen to the Yanomami? Why?

E Comprehension: True/False/No Information

_____ 1. The Yanomami live in a tropical forest.
_____ 2. The Venezuelan and Brazilian governments want to help the Yanomami.
_____ 3. Today the Yanomami know they live in South America.
_____ 4. The Yanomami live peacefully.
_____ 5. We call them Stone Age people because they used stone tools.
_____ 6. Scientists study the Yanomami because they hunt with stone axes.
_____ 7. They ate plants and animals.
_____ 8. Yanomami villages are usually good friends with each other.
_____ 9. The Yanomami are afraid of new things.
_____ 10. Mining companies are opening schools for the Yanomami.
_____ 11. We could learn something from the Yanomami.

F Main Idea

1. The Yanomami were Stone Age people, but now their lives are changing very fast.
2. The Yanomami live in the tropical forest near the Amazon River, but they know nothing about other South Americans.
3. The modern world is teaching the Yanomami to live in peace.

The Hopi of Arizona

LESSON

Pre-reading Questions

1. Does this man have modern things?
2. Describe his clothes.
3. What is the building behind this man?

The Hopi of Arizona

The Hopi live in the northeastern part of
Arizona in the United States. The United States
is a very modern country. Tall buildings,
highways, computers, and hundreds of other
5 modern things are a part of every American's
life. **Somehow,** with modern things all around
them, the Hopi keep their traditions.

There are about ten thousand (10,000)
Hopi and they live in twelve villages in the
10 desert. The weather is very hot in summer, but
in winter it **freezes.** The wind **blows** hard.
Farming is difficult.

Corn is the Hopi's main food, but they
plant vegetables too. They raise sheep, **goats,**
15 and cattle. They also eat hamburgers and ice
cream and drink soft drinks. They live in
traditional stone houses, but many of them
have telephones, radios, and television. They
have horses, but they have **pickup trucks** too.

20 **Kachinas** are an important part of the
Hopi religion. Kachinas are **spirits** of **dead**
people, of **rocks,** plants, and animals, and of the
stars. Men dress as kachinas and do religious
dances. People also make wooden kachinas. No
25 two wooden kachinas are **ever** alike.

The children attend school and learn
English and other subjects. A few Hopi go to

goat

in some way

goes below 0°C

pickup truck

dead = adjective for *die*

stones

not ever = never

kachina

universities. Some of the adults live and work
in nearby towns.

30   The children attend school, and they also
learn the Hopi language, dances, and stories.
The Hopi want a comfortable, modern life, but
they don't want to **lose** their traditions.   verb for *lost*

A Vocabulary

somehow	ever	rocks	lose
blows	goats	kachinas	dead
freezes	pickup trucks	cattle	spirits

1. The wind _____ hard.
2. They have horses, but they have _____ too.
3. _____ are an important part of their religion.
4. The Hopi want a comfortable, modern life, but they don't want to
   _____ their traditions.
5. _____, with modern things all around them, the Hopi
   keep their traditions.
6. Kachinas are _____ of _____ people, of
   _____, plants, and animals, and of the stars.
7. No two wooden kachinas are _____ alike.
8. They raise sheep, _____, and cattle.
9. The weather is very hot in summer, but in winter it _____.

B Vocabulary (new context)

pickup	dead	lose	goats
somehow	television	freezes	spirits
nearby	blowing	ever	religious

1. Young people can _____ understand the words in rap
   videos.
2. Some African villagers say that trees have _____.
3. Don't be nervous. It is only the wind _____.
4. Most cowboys have a _____ truck and a horse.
5. Some people like to eat meat from _____.

6. President John F. Kennedy died in 1963. He is _____.
7. Water _____ at 0°C and changes into ice.
8. Our band cannot _____ play softly. It always plays loudly.
9. Did you _____ your pen? Is it lost?

C Vocabulary Review

deep	skiing	trip	nomads
tent	sled	wavy	uncomfortable
attend	beard	complete	continues
cards	dark	reach	beat

1. Russians traveled by _____ in winter before they had cars and buses.
2. Let's play a game of _____. I don't feel like studying.
3. Riding for hours on a motorcycle is _____.
4. David's parents took a _____ to South America last year.
5. The Mississippi River is very _____ in some places.
6. _____ in Central Asia take their sheep into the mountains in summer.
7. Are you planning to _____ the dance next Saturday?
8. The story on some television programs _____ from one week to the next.
9. Ruth and Ann are going camping in the mountains. They have a _____ to sleep in.
10. Oscar didn't have time to _____ his composition before the bell rang.
11. Howard has _____ blond hair and a short _____.
12. Did you ever go _____ in Switzerland in the winter?

D Questions

1. Where do the Hopi live?
2. What things are a part of every American's life?
3. What is the weather like in the Hopi villages?
4. What is their main food?

*5. What kind of meat do they eat?
6. Do they eat food that other Americans eat?
7. What is modern about some of their homes? What is traditional?
8. Where do the children learn English?
9. What are kachinas?
10. Why do they teach their children the language, dances, and stories?
*11. Are Hopi children more like Sami or Ainu children? Why?

E Comprehension

1. The Hopi live in the state of _____.
   a. Utah   c. Arizona
   b. New Mexico   d. New York

2. The Hopi _____.
   a. want modern things instead of traditional ones
   b. want traditional things instead of modern ones
   c. don't want to remember their traditions
   d. want both modern and traditional things

3. Winters in this part of Arizona are _____.
   a. hot   c. cool
   b. warm   d. cold

4. The main Hopi food is _____.
   a. corn   c. beef
   b. hamburgers   d. vegetables

*5. A pickup truck is useful for people _____.
   a. in a city apartment   c. in New York City
   b. on a farm   d. near an airport

*6. The Hopi probably eat _____ sometimes.
   a. frogs   c. potato chips and pizza
   b. polar bears   d. reindeer meat

7. Kachinas are _____.
   a. men   c. animals
   b. something to eat   d. spirits

8. The Hopi don't want to ———— their traditions.
   a. lose   c. remember
   b. hit   d. learn

F Main Idea

1. The Hopi raise crops and animals in the Arizona desert.
2. Kachinas are spirits of the things around the Hopi.
3. The Hopi keep their traditions even with modern life all around them.

The Maori of New Zealand

LESSON

Pre-reading Questions

1. Do these people live alone or in groups?

2. Describe the building in the picture.

3. What is in front of the building? How do the people use it?

The Maori of New Zealand

Polynesians live on islands in the Pacific Ocean. The Maori are Polynesians and they live at the southern end of Polynesia in New Zealand. There are about 280,000 Maori today.

5   Maori, like other Polynesians, have brown skin, dark brown eyes, and wavy black hair. Men have beards and mustaches, but they usually **shave** them.

shave

The Maori **arrived** in New Zealand from
10 other Polynesian islands **over** a thousand years ago. They were the first people to live there. They made beautiful wooden buildings with pictures cut into the wood.

came

more than

There was one terrible thing about their
15 life. They fought wars **among themselves** for several centuries. Then British people came to live there in the 1790s, and some of the Maori fought them. In 1840 they **agreed** to become a British **colony.** This brought peace to the coun-
20 try. When they stopped fighting, they learned European ways quickly.

between

Today there are Maori in all kinds of jobs. They attend schools and universities and become lawyers and scientists. There are Maori
25 in the government. Most of them live like the white New Zealanders.

However, the Maori do not forget their traditions. Children learn the language, music, and old stories. They have **yearly** competitions   every year

30 in speaking, dancing, and singing. They **practice** for months. Then all the Maori in the area arrive to watch the competitions and see who **wins.** They also visit old friends.

Today the Maori live a comfortable, modern

35 life. However, they are not losing their traditions because they pass them on to their children.

A Vocabulary

among	islands	yearly	over
wins	competitions	arrived	themselves
practice	colony	shave	agreed

1. The Maori _____ in New Zealand from other Polynesian islands _____ a thousand years ago.
2. They have _____ _____ in speaking, dancing, and singing.
3. Men have beards and mustaches, but they usually _____ them.
4. They fought wars _____ _____ for several centuries.
5. In 1840 they _____ to become a British _____ .
6. They _____ for months.
7. Then all the Maori in the area arrive to watch the competitions and see who _____ .

B Vocabulary (new context)

arrive	yearly	practice	wins
competition	themselves	colony	over
shave	among	agree	passing

1. The children made lunch _____ because their parents weren't home.
2. You should _____ your English outside of class. Speak English _____ yourselves between classes.

3. There is a sports _____ this week. Students from six universities are coming.
4. I think that the Sami nomads have a very hard life. Do you _____?
5. What time does your plane _____ in Chicago?
6. Some men have to _____ every day.
7. Brazil was a Portuguese _____.
8. English teachers go to a _____ meeting. They go every year.
9. The Ainu arrived in Japan _____ 7,000 years ago.
10. Every year our city _____ the music competition.

C Vocabulary Review

Match the words that mean the same.

Column A
1. not ever _____
2. freeze _____
3. perhaps _____
4. dead _____
5. less _____
6. attend _____
7. somehow _____
8. travel _____
9. thick _____
10. desert _____

Column B
a. not alive
b. in some way
c. a dry area
d. never
e. take a trip
f. fewer
g. change to ice
h. computer
i. go to
j. not thin
k. maybe

D Questions

1. Where do Polynesians live?
*2. Where is New Zealand?
3. How many Maori are there?
4. What do the Maori look like?
5. Where did the Maori come from?
6. What was terrible about their life?
7. Why did they agree to become a British colony?
8. Do the Maori attend universities?
9. How do most Maori live today?
10. What do they do at their yearly competitions?
*11. How are the Maori and Ainu alike?

E   Comprehension: True/False

_____ *1. Today the Maori probably wear traditional clothes.
_____ 2. The Maori are Polynesians.
_____ 3. New Zealand is an island country.
_____ 4. The Maori look like the Chinese.
_____ 5. When the Maori arrived in New Zealand, they fought with the other people there.
_____ 6. The Maori wanted peace in their country.
_____ 7. The Maori live by hunting and fishing.
_____ *8. There are probably Maori teachers.
_____ 9. The Maori like music.
_____ *10. The Maori teach their children to fight wars against the white people.

F   Main Idea

Write the numbers of the supporting ideas under the right names. Some may go under more than one name.

Sami	Ainu	Yanomami	Hopi	Maori

1. They live on an island.
2. They are very violent.
3. They live in a grass house with a dirt floor.
4. They have stone houses.
5. They live part of the year in tents.
6. They were the first people on their island.
7. They had only stone tools.
8. Corn is their main food.
9. They eat reindeer meat.
10. They have farms.
11. They live in the desert.
12. They live in the far north.
13. There are only a few of them left.
14. They need warm clothes.
15. They live in the tropical forest.
16. Their traditions will probably die.

Word Study

A -self Pronouns (Reflexive Pronouns)

A mirror **reflects. Reflexive** pronouns reflect on the subject of the sentence.

Example: **You** see **yourself** in the mirror.
The Maori fought wars among **themselves.**
I don't need any help. **I** can do it **myself.**

Subject Pronoun	Reflexive Pronoun
I	myself
you	yourself
he	himself
she	herself
it	itself
we	ourselves
you	yourselves
they	themselves

Put the right *-self* pronoun in the blanks.

1. We usually speak English among _____ at the Student Union.
2. No one can practice English for you. You have to do it
   _____ .
3. You should practice among _____ .
4. The officials agreed among _____ .
5. A modern elevator moves by _____ when someone pushes the button.
6. The computer specialist usually does her work by
   _____ .
7. No one told me about it. I saw it _____ .
8. Carlos taught _____ how to speak English.

B Superlatives

When we compare two things or people, we use the comparative forms **-er than, more than, better, worse,** or **farther.**

When we compare three or more things or people, we use **the** + adjective + **-est** with words of one syllable.

    Example: Tom is **the oldest** student in the class.

We use **the most** + adjective with words of three or more syllables.

    Example: Ann is **the most intelligent** student in the class.

    Irregular: good – better than – the best
                        bad   – worse than – the worst
                        far   – farther than – the farthest

    Example: Ann is **the best** student in the class.
                        Sarah is **the worst** student in the class.
                        Mary ran **the farthest.**

    Spelling: Use the **1-1-1** rule.

                     big – biggest

Put the superlative form of the adjective in the blank. Use *the*.

(beautiful) 1. Switzerland is _____ country in Europe.

(expensive) 2. A Rolls Royce is _____ kind of car in the world.

(good) 3. This morning Kumiko wrote _____ composition that she ever wrote.

(tall) 4. Who is _____ student in the class?

(important) 5. Rice is _____ food for millions of people.

(far) 6. Who drives _____ to come to class?

(bad) 7. The _____ fires burn toxic substances.

(dark) 8. Black is _____ color.

(strong) 9. Who is _____ person in your family?

C Word Forms

	Verb	Noun	Adjective
1.	use	use	useful
2.		tropics	tropical
3.	sweeten	sweetener	sweet
4.	mix	mixture	
5.	weigh	weight	
6.	fill		full
7.		tradition	traditional
8.		wood	wooden
9.		religion	religious
10.		noise	noisy

**Put the right word form in each blank. Choose a word form from Line 1
for Sentence 1. Choose a word form from Line 2 for Sentence 2, and so on.**

1. A metal knife is very _____ for the Yanomami.
2. Northern Brazil is a _____ area.
3. You can _____ your tea with some sugar.
4. An ice cream soda is a _____ of ice cream and a cola.
5. How much does a compact disc _____?
6. His coffee cup is _____.
7. Music is an important Maori _____.
8. Hopi do not live in _____ houses.
9. What is your _____?
10. Some children are very _____.

D Irregular Verbs

1. Memorize these verb forms. Then use the past tense of each verb in
   a sentence.

	Simple	Past		Simple	Past
a.	do	did	f.	blow	blew
b.	have	had	g.	know	knew
c.	ring	rang	h.	hit	hit
d.	begin	began	i.	tell	told
e.	sweep	swept	j.	win	won

2. **Write the past tense of these verbs.**

a. become ——————
b. buy ——————
c. bring ——————
d. cut ——————
e. come ——————
f. find ——————

g. fight ——————
h. go ——————
i. get ——————
j. see ——————
k. teach ——————
l. win ——————

E Writing

Write real information in your answers.

1. You have to go to live with one of the groups of people in *Unit 6* for one year. Who do you want to live with? Why?
2. Which group of people in *Unit 6* do you **not** want to live with? Why not?
3. In what ways is modern life good for traditional people? In what ways is it bad for them?

Video Highlights

A Before You Watch

1. You have read about the Hopi people of Arizona. Write down two facts that you already know about the Hopi.

   a. _____

   b. _____

2. These words will help you understand the video. Read the words and their definitions.

   Congress— In the USA, a government group that makes new laws.
   dispute— a disagreement or argument.
   Navajo— a group of Native Americans who live in parts of Utah, Arizona, and New Mexico.
   Reservation—land that is set aside for Native Americans to live on.

   Now choose one of the key words above for each of these sentences:

   a. Many Native Americans in the United States and Canada live on a

   _____.

   b. When two groups of people do not agree about something, they are having a _____.

   c. The members of _____ often disagree about what is best for the country.

   d. The Hopi and the _____ both live in the south-western part of the United States.

©CNN

215

B As You Watch

Two groups of people, the Hopi and the landowners, want the same land. As you watch the video, complete each of the following sentences.

a. The _____ want the land so they can use it for hiking, bicycling, and camping.

b. The _____ want the land because it is theirs historically. It is also very sacred to them.

C After You Watch

1. Read the following passages. Fill in the blanks with information from the video.

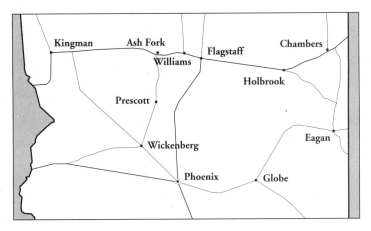

a. The landowners in the video are Americans. They live in _____. They own _____ and businesses there. Some of them, like Bob Alexander, live on _____ land. This sacred land belonged to the Hopi long ago. The landowners do want the _____ to control the land again. They are afraid they will lose everything.

b. The Hopi are a group of Native Americans. They live in Arizona, in communities called *pueblos*. The Hopi are peaceful. They are _____ and sheepherders. They also have exciting ceremonies. One famous ritual is called the _____ Dance. The dancers perform with live snakes in their _____ .

2. Discuss: Who do you think the land should belong to? Why?

Activity Page

A Compare Groups

Using the diagram below as an example, complete the exercise.
Write facts that are *only* true for the Ainu people of Japan in the left circle.
Write facts that are *only* true for the Maori people of New Zealand in the
  right circle.

AINU   MAORI

Live in Japan   *have wavy hair*   *live in New Zealand*

Write facts that are true for *both* of the groups of people in the middle.

a. eat seafood

b. have beards and mustaches

c. live a modern life

d. hunt brown bears

e. have brown eyes

f. make houses from grass

g. grow rice

h. build wooden buildings

B Who Am I?

You and a partner choose roles. Partner A is the interviewer. Partner B
chooses a culture from Lessons 1–5. Partner B pretends to be a person from
that culture. The interviewer asks Partner B questions about his or her culture. Continue until Partner A knows Partner B's culture.

Example:
A: Where are you from?
B: I am from Norway.
A: Where do you live?
B: In the mountains.
A: What kind of house do you live in?
B: I live in a tent made of reindeer skin. Do you know who I am?
A: Yes, you are a Sami from Norway.

Dictionary Page

Understanding Definitions

Words often have more than one meaning. Read all of the different meanings of the noun *light*.

light /laɪt/ *noun*
1 *(no plural)* energy from the sun, electric lights, fire, etc., that allows us to see
2 *(no plural)* sunshine, daylight: *He walked out of the house and into the light.*
3 something that produces light, such as light bulbs or lamps: *When it is dark, we turn on the lights.*
4 something that can start a fire, such as a match: *She took out a cigarette and asked her friend for a light.*
5 a traffic signal: *Turn right at the next light.*
6 a way of understanding: *He now looks back on his life and sees it in a new light.*
to make light of: to treat as if unimportant: *He made light of his illness, but we knew it was serious.*
light *verb* **lighted** or **lit** /lɪt/, **lighting, lights**
1 to set on fire: *We light a fire in the fireplace on cold winter nights.*

to light up: a. to brighten, as with happiness: *Her eyes lit up at the good news.*
b. to make a cigarette burn
light *adjective* **lighter, lightest**
1 having little weight, not heavy: *An empty suitcase is light.*
2 pale in color, not dark: *She wore a light blue dress.*
3 not forceful, or strong: *a light rain, a light sleep*
4 gentle, delicate: *Dancers move with light steps. See:* art on page 23a.
light bulb *noun*
the round glass part of an electric light
lighter /ˈlaɪtər/ *adjective*
comparative of light:
not as heavy in weight or dark in color as something else: *A feather is lighter than a rock.||White is lighter than gray.*

light bulb

Now read each of the following sentences. How is the word used in each sentence? Which definition is it? Write the number of the definition next to each sentence.

Example: __3__ Please turn out the *lights* before you leave.

1. _____ Excuse me, do you have a *light?*
2. _____ I hope we'll get there while it's still *light* outside.
3. _____ The *light* was shining down through the trees.
4. _____ The speeding car did not stop for the red *light.*
5. _____ After Dennis listened to the Hopi side of the story, he understood the dispute in a completely different *light.*

Exploration and Adventure

Context Clues

1. Captain James Cook was a famous English **explorer.** He was the first European to visit most of the Pacific islands.
   a. a place that has water all around it
   b. a businessman who travels to different countries
   c. a person who looks for new places and information about them
   d. a ship that travels to new places

2. Captain Cook's ship had **sailors** on it, because there is a lot of work on a ship.
   a. men who do the work on a ship
   b. men who live in colonies
   c. people in competitions
   d. people who travel on ships during their vacation

3. There **might** be a quiz on Friday. If we don't finish the lesson Thursday, the quiz will be Monday.
   a. will   c. perhaps
   b. is going to   d. was

4. Ruth had to study the **history** of Europe in school. She learned about wars, kings, governments, religion, and everything that happened there.
   a. the mountains, rivers, and lakes
   b. the countries, cities, and towns
   c. scientists and the things they invent
   d. everything that happened in the past

5. Abdullah always gets good grades on his tests, so I **suppose** he will get a good grade on this one too.
   a. think   c. want
   b. dinner   d. have to

6. Helen's family and friends had a party and gave her **gifts** on her twenty-first birthday.
   a. $100   c. food
   b. presents   d. cattle

7. Helen was very **pleased** when she saw the gifts.
   a. unhappy
   b. deep
   c. afraid
   d. happy

8. A hippopotamus is **heavy.** A spider is not **heavy.**
   a. deep
   b. very tall
   c. weighs a lot
   d. has six legs

9. Masako was playing basketball and she **injured** her arm. She went to the doctor and cannot play again for six months.
   a. hurt
   b. told
   c. arrived
   d. won

10. Masako's arm is better now. She is **glad** that she can play basketball again.
    a. hurt
    b. dead
    c. happy
    d. jump

11. I found a writing book, but it has no name in it. Who does it **belong to?**
    a. Where is it?
    b. Whose is it?
    c. What is it?
    d. When is it?

12. Dan is three years old. He is **able to** walk and talk, but he can't read or write.
    a. can
    b. has to
    c. wants to
    d. plans to

13. This television program is one hour long. It starts at 8:00 and is **over** at 9:00.
    a. wonderful
    b. double
    c. finished
    d. middle

14. The Amazon River area is in the tropics. Many kinds of animals live in the **jungle** there.
    a. desert
    b. tropical forest
    c. ice and snow
    d. towns

The Polynesians

LESSON

1

Pre-reading Questions

1. How do these people travel?

2. Is it warm or cold where they live?

3. Why is wind important to these people?

1

The Polynesians

The Polynesians were probably the best **explorers** in the **history** of the world. They traveled thousands of kilometers across the Pacific Ocean in large **double canoes.** They could look
5 at the stars and know which way to go. They also understood the wind and ocean **currents.** They made **maps** of the stars and ocean currents. They made these maps out of sticks and **shells.**

About four thousand years ago a group of
10 people lived in southern China. They were a mixture of white, black, and Mongol people. When the Chinese moved farther and farther into the south, these people needed to find **safer** homes.

Slowly these Polynesians left China in
15 their double canoes and started toward the southeast. They took animals and plants with them. A group of people **might** arrive at an island and stay there until they had children, grandchildren, and great-grandchildren. Then a
20 few families might start traveling again. Some canoes went one way and some another. It took hundreds of years for them to reach all of the islands in Polynesia.

The Polynesian double canoe is one of the
25 **greatest** inventions in history. The Polynesians were among the greatest **sailors** in history. They understood how to sail by the stars, wind, and ocean currents. This made them great explorers.

rivers in the ocean

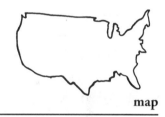

map

less dangerous

would maybe

shells

best, most wonderful

A Vocabulary

explorers	safer	history	maps
greatest	grandchildren	sailors	double
shells	canoes	might	currents

1. The Polynesian double canoe is one of the _____ inventions in history.
2. When the Chinese moved farther and farther into the south, these people needed to find _____ homes.
3. The Polynesians were probably the best _____ in the _____ of the world.
4. A group of people _____ arrive at an island and stay there until they had children, grandchildren, and great-grandchildren.
5. The Polynesians were among the greatest _____ in history.
6. They also understood the wind and ocean _____.
7. They traveled thousands of miles across the Pacific Ocean in large _____ _____.
8. They made _____ of the stars and ocean currents.
9. They made these maps out of sticks and _____.

B Vocabulary (new context)

southeast	shell	might	history
safe	great	double	map
sailor	explorer	current	canoe

1. Madame Curie was a _____ scientist.
2. Children study the _____ of their country.
3. We _____ go to Los Angeles for our vacation, but we are not sure.
4. A warm ocean _____ off the coast of Norway makes Norway warmer than Sweden.
5. A _____ works on a ship.
6. Can you find Polynesia on the _____?
7. It isn't _____ for little children to play alone in a swimming pool.
8. A _____ is a small sea animal's house.
9. If you _____ three, you get six.

10. Marco Polo was a great _____. He crossed Asia and lived in China for several years in the thirteenth century.
11. Some North American people traveled by _____.

C Vocabulary Review

relaxing	country	cassette	calmer
temperature	jumped	enough	shape
yet	silk	enter	bell
Age	official	metal	frog

1. Some people work in town but do not enjoy city life. They like to live out in the _____.
2. The students are _____ under a tree.
3. You don't have _____ time to have lunch before your next class.
4. Did the 10:00 _____ ring _____? I didn't hear it.
5. The sixteenth century was the _____ of Exploration for Europeans.
6. The _____ in New Zealand is lower than in Hawaii.
7. Polynesia is in the _____ of a triangle (Δ).
8. Three frogs _____ into the water.
9. Is your nephew going to _____ the sports competition?

D Questions

1. What did the Polynesians travel in?
2. How did they know which way to go?
3. What did they make their maps from?
4. Where did Polynesians come from in the beginning?
5. Why did they leave China?
6. What did they take with them?
7. Did they travel different ways across the ocean?
8. How long did it take for them to reach all of Polynesia?
9. What made the Polynesians great explorers?
*10. Are ocean currents important for ships today? Why?
*11. Are the stars important for ships today? Why?

■E■ Comprehension: True/False/No Information

_____ 1. Hawaiians are Polynesians.
_____ 2. Maori are Polynesians.
_____ 3. Polynesians came from southern China.
_____ 4. Polynesians are a mixture of different groups of people.
_____ 5. They traveled from one group of islands to another very quickly.
_____ 6. They took dogs with them from China.
_____ 7. Some people died on the way to new islands.
_____ 8. The Polynesian double canoe is a great invention.
_____ 9. The Polynesians were great sailors and explorers.
_____ 10. They made maps on paper.

■F■ Main Idea

1. The Polynesians left China and became some of the greatest explorers in history.
2. The Polynesians went from China to hundreds of Pacific Islands.
3. The Polynesians invented the double canoe.

A Giraffe in Central Asia

LESSON

Pre-reading Questions

1. What is this animal?
2. Where does it live? Is it from Asia?
3. Is it used to walking a long way in the desert?

A Giraffe in Central Asia

Tamerlane (1336?–1405) was a very strong Mongol **leader.** He and his soldiers fought until Tamerlane became the **ruler** of all Central Asia. Other countries wanted to make friends with
5 Tamerlane. It was safer to be friends than enemies.

Ambassadors from many countries took **gifts** to Tamerlane. They took beautiful cloth, **jewelry, gold** (Au), and **silver** (Ag). They often tried to take something unusual as a gift too.

10 In 1404, near the end of Tamerlane's life, an Egyptian ambassador arrived in Samarkand. This was where Tamerlane lived. The ambassador and his men traveled on horses and camels. They brought a **giraffe** from Africa as a gift.

15 Egyptian camels and horses were **used to** walking in the desert. They did it all the time. A giraffe is not used to the desert. But this giraffe walked 5,000 kilometers from Cairo to Samarkand.

20 We know about the Egyptian ambassador's gift because several people wrote about it. No one wrote that Tamerlane like it. However, we **suppose** that he was very **pleased** to have this strange African animal in Central Asia.

jewelry

presents

suppose = think, guess/pleased = happy

A Vocabulary

make friends	used to	leader	suppose
ambassadors	ruler	pleased	silver
jewelry	gifts	gold	giraffe

1. _____ from many countries took _____ to Tamerlane.
2. Egyptian camels and horses were _____ walking in the desert.
3. Tamerlane (1336?–1405) was a very strong Mongol _____.
4. They took beautiful cloth, _____, _____ (Au), and _____ (Ag).
5. However, we _____ that he was very _____ to have this strange African animal in Central Asia.
6. He and his soldiers fought until Tamerlane was the _____ of all of Central Asia.
7. They brought a _____ from Africa as a gift.

B Vocabulary (new context)

giraffe	leader	jewelry	soldiers
supposed	gold	ruler	pleased
used to	silver	gifts	ambassador

1. Who is your country's _____ to the United States?
2. A _____ has a very long neck.
3. _____ jewelry is expensive. _____ jewelry is less expensive than gold.
4. Some women like to wear a lot of _____.
5. Masako is never absent from class, but she is not here today. I _____ she is sick.
6. A king is the _____ of a country. He is also the _____ of his people.
7. When Japanese students study in the United States, they can't get _____ the food because it is very strange.
8. Ali got an excellent grade on his quiz. He was _____.
9. Americans usually get _____ on their birthday.

C Vocabulary Review

Match the words that mean the opposite.

Column A

1. arrive _____
2. safe _____
3. inside _____
4. fans _____
5. start _____
6. dead _____
7. lose _____
8. higher _____
9. more _____
10. somebody _____

Column B

a. performers
b. fewer
c. find
d. leave
e. outside
f. dangerous
g. great
h. lower
i. stop
j. yearly
k. alive
l. nobody

D Questions

*1. What does the question mark mean in (1336?–1405)?
2. Who was Tamerlane?
3. Why did other countries want to make friends with him?
*4. Why did ambassadors take gifts to Tamerlane?
5. What kind of gifts did they take?
*6. Why did they often try to take something unusual?
7. Who took a giraffe to Tamerlane?
8. How did the giraffe get to Samarkand?
*9. Do you think Tamerlane liked the giraffe? Why?

E Comprehension

1. Tamerlane was _____ leader.
   a. an Egyptian   c. a Mongol
   b. a Chinese   d. an Arab

2. Tamerlane became the ruler of Central Asia because of _____.
   a. ambassadors   c. enemies
   b. wars   d. gifts

3. Other countries wanted to _____ friends with Tamerlane.
   a. make   c. buy
   b. give   d. find

4. Ag means _____.
   a. jewelry   c. gold
   b. gifts   d. silver

5. A giraffe was _____ gift.
   a. an unusual   c. a double
   b. a safe   d. a dead

6. Giraffes are not _____ walking in the desert.
   a. arrived   c. used to
   b. bought   d. wrote

7. Tamerlane was probably _____ to have this unusual animal.
   a. strong   c. safer
   b. dangerous   d. pleased

F Main Idea

1. An Egyptian ambassador took a giraffe to Tamerlane.
2. Tamerlane was a strong Mongol ruler of Central Asia.
3. Ambassadors took beautiful and unusual gifts to Tamerlane.

The First Woman on Mount Everest

LESSON 3

Pre-reading Questions

1. Where is Mount Everest?
2. Do you know any mountain climbers?
3. Do you like to climb mountains?

3

The First Woman on Mount Everest

Mount Everest is the highest mountain in the world. It is in the Himalayan Mountains between Nepal and China, and it is 8,900 meters high. Sir Edmund Hillary from New
5 Zealand and Tenzing Norgay from Nepal were the first people ever to climb Mount Everest. They climbed it in 1953. Men from several different countries climbed it after that.

Junko Tabei, a Japanese from Hokkaido,
10 was the first woman to make this difficult climb. A Tokyo newspaper-television company **organized** the Mount Everest climb in 1975. They **chose** fifteen women from mountaineering **clubs** to go to Nepal. The group climbed
15 for several days. Then there was an **avalanche.** The **heavy** ice and snow **injured** ten of the women. They had to stop climbing. The other five continued.

Only Ms. Tabei **was able** to climb the last
20 70 meters. She was standing on top of the world. She was the first woman there.

Ms. Tabei was 35 years old at the time. She started climbing mountains in 1960. She **still** climbs mountains. She is not an **ordinary**
25 Japanese housewife. Her husband works for Honda Motor Company. He likes to climb

planned
past tense of *choose*

hurt

could

in the past and now

mountains, too. But he can't have enough vacation from his work to go with his wife all the time. So he stays home to take care of the
30 house and children.

Ms. Tabei earns money for her trips by teaching English and piano to children. She also speaks to groups of people about her mountain climbing. She climbs a mountain
35 about every three years. She climbed the highest mountains on six continents. **Finally,** she wants to climb the highest mountain in every country in the world. When she reaches the top of a mountain, she thinks, "I'm **glad** that I'm at the
40 top." Then she climbs back down.

<small>happy</small>

A Vocabulary

injured	ordinary	kilograms	finally
heavy	was able	still	organized
glad	avalanche	chose	clubs

1. They _____ fifteen women from mountaineering _____ to go to Nepal.
2. Only Ms. Tabei _____ to climb the last 70 meters.
3. She _____ climbs mountains.
4. A Tokyo newspaper-television company _____ the Mount Everest climb in 1975.
5. She is not an _____ Japanese housewife.
6. The _____ ice and snow _____ ten of the women.
7. When she reaches the top of a mountain, she thinks, "I'm _____ that I'm at the top."
8. Then there was an _____.
9. _____, she wants to climb the highest mountain in every country in the world.

B   Vocabulary (new context)

highest	injured	finally	organize
able	glad	still	heavier
ordinary	choose	Club	climb

1. The water spider is not an _____ spider. It is very unusual because it lives under water.
2. Abdullah took the TOEFL test four times. _____, he passed it. He was not _____ to pass it the first three times. He is very _____ that he passed it.
3. If you need a new shirt, you go to a store. You _____ a shirt and buy it.
4. The students are going to _____ a party for the last day of classes.
5. A hippopotamus is _____ than a camel.
6. Robert _____ his leg while he was skiing.
7. The International Student _____ is going to have a dance on Saturday night.

C   Vocabulary Review

Match the words that mean the same.

Column A
1. gift _____
2. pleased _____
3. great _____
4. among _____
5. leader _____
6. completely _____
7. fewer _____
8. pretty _____
9. suppose _____
10. perhaps _____
11. cattle _____

Column B
a. maybe
b. between
c. think
d. ruler
e. shave
f. wonderful
g. sled
h. present
i. cows
j. less
k. glad
l. all
m. beautiful

D Questions

1. When did the first mountain climbers reach the top of Mount Everest?
2. Where is Mount Everest?
3. Is Mount Everest an ordinary mountain? Why?
4. Who was the first woman to climb Mount Everest?
5. Who organized the climb?
6. What happened to ten of the women climbers?
7. Is Mount Everest the only mountain Ms. Tabei climbed?
*8. Why isn't Ms. Tabei an ordinary Japanese housewife?
9. Why does Ms. Tabei's husband stay at home to take care of the house and children?
10. What does Ms. Tabei do when she reaches the top of a mountain?
*11. How does Ms. Tabei pay for her mountain climbing? Is it expensive?
*12. Will Ms. Tabei stop climbing mountains soon?

E Comprehension

*1. When people climb Mount Everest, most of them start in _____.
   a. China   c. India
   b. New Zealand   d. Nepal

2. Two people climbed Mount Everest in 1953. They were from _____.
   a. Japan   c. Nepal
   b. New Zealand   d. b and c

3. _____ Japanese women started to climb Mount Everest.
   a. One   c. Two
   b. Five   d. Fifteen

4. A company in _____ organized the climb.
   a. Tokyo   c. Nepal
   b. Hokkaido   d. New Zealand

5. _____ injured ten of the women.
   a. A club   c. An avalanche
   b. An ordinary   d. A storm

6. Junko Tabei's age was ———— when she climbed the highest mountain in the world.
   a. 25   c. 35
   b. 30   d. 40

7. Ms. Tabei practiced climbing for ———— years before she climbed Mount Everest.
   a. 15   c. 30
   b. 25   d. 40

*8. When Ms. Tabei climbs all the high mountains in the world, she will feel ————.
   a. afraid   c. glad
   b. sad   d. b and c

F Main Idea

1. Mount Everest is the highest mountain in the world.
2. Junko Tabei, an unusual Japanese housewife, climbs many high mountains.
3. Junko Tabei was glad when she reached the top of Mount Everest.

The European Raja
of Sarawak

LESSON

Pre-reading Questions

1. Where is Sarawak?

2. Is Sarawak near Europe?

3. What do they call the leader of
   Sarawak?

The European Raja of Sarawak

James Brooke (1803–1868) was born in India. However, he was British, not Indian. India was a British colony at that time, and James's father was an official in the colonial
5 government.

James attended school in England, and then he went into the army. He was injured in a war in Burma, so he left the army. He bought a boat and explored the islands off the coast of
10 Asia.

Sarawak is on one of these islands. The name of the island is Kalimantan. Today most of Kalimantan **belongs to** Indonesia. While Mr. Brooke was traveling in Asia, there were
15 problems in Sarawak. Some of the people did not like their leader, the **raja,** so they started fighting against him. The fighting continued and the raja couldn't stop it. Finally, he asked Mr. Brooke for help.

20 Mr Brooke asked the British **navy** to help him. They soon **defeated** the raja's enemies. When the war was **over,** the raja asked Mr.   finished
Brooke to be the ruler of Sarawak. He became the raja. It was very unusual to have a
25 European raja in Asia.

He was a good ruler. He organized a strong government, and there was no more fighting. Some of the people in the **jungle**   tropical forest
were head hunters. They killed people and
30 kept their heads. He made them stop.

After James Brooke's **death**, his son   noun for *die*
became raja.

Today Sarawak is part of Malaysia.
Malaysia is an **independent** country instead of
35 a British colony. Sarawak has a **governor,** but
he is not British. There are no more British
rulers in Sarawak or Malaysia.

A Vocabulary

belongs to	jungle	colonial	death
Kalimantan	governor	problems	navy
raja	independent	over	defeated

1. Sarawak has a _____, but he is not British.
2. Some of the people did not like their leader, the _____.
3. Mr. Brooke asked the British to help him.
4. Today most of Kalimantan _____ Indonesia.
5. Malaysia is an _____ country instead of a British colony.
6. They soon _____ the raja's enemies.
7. After James Brooke's _____, his son became raja.
8. When the war was _____, the raja asked Mr. Brooke to be the ruler of Sarawak.
9. Some of the people in the _____ were head hunters.

B Vocabulary (new context)

defeated	death	belong to	jungle
governor	navy	against	over
attend	colonial	independent	Sarawak

1. The Yanomami live in the _____ near the Amazon.

2. Every state in the United States has a _____.
3. Our university _____ the only other university in the ball game last night.
4. Gary is in the army. His brother is a sailor in the _____.
5. The class begins at 11:00. It is _____ at 11:50.
6. Elizabeth II became queen after the _____ of her father.
7. Who does this jacket _____? I found it in our classroom yesterday.
8. All of the old colonies in Africa are _____ countries now.

C Vocabulary Review

Underline the word that does not belong.

1. double, once, twice, two
2. going to, might, maybe, perhaps
3. giraffe, hippo, camel, spider
4. agree, pleased, glad, happy
5. see, teach, explore, ring
6. yearly, completely, monthly, weekly
7. heavy, thick, gift, ordinary
8. middle, common, ordinary, usual
9. best, worst, oldest, farthest

D Questions

1. When did James Brooke die?
*2. What century did he live in?
3. Was he Indian?
4. What did he do after he finished school?
5. Why did he leave the army?
6. What did he do after he left the army?
7. Where is Sarawak?
8. What were the problems in Sarawak?
*9. Why did the raja ask Mr. Brooke to become the ruler?
10. Was Mr. Brooke a good ruler?
11. Is Sarawak a colony today?

E Comprehension: Sequence

Number these sentences in the right order.

_____ Mr. Brooke defeated the raja's enemies.

_____ Mr. Brooke went to England to study.

_____ Mr. Brooke became the raja of Sarawak.

_____ Sarawak became part of Malaysia.

_____ Mr. Brooke was injured.

_____ Mr. Brooke organized a strong government.

___1___ James Brooke was born in India.

_____ Mr. Brooke died in 1868.

_____ Some of the people fought against the raja.

_____ Mr. Brooke's son became raja.

F Main Idea

1. James Brooke was English, but he was born in India.
2. An Englishman became the raja of an Asian country.
3. James Brooke was a good ruler, and he organized a strong government.

The Iditarod

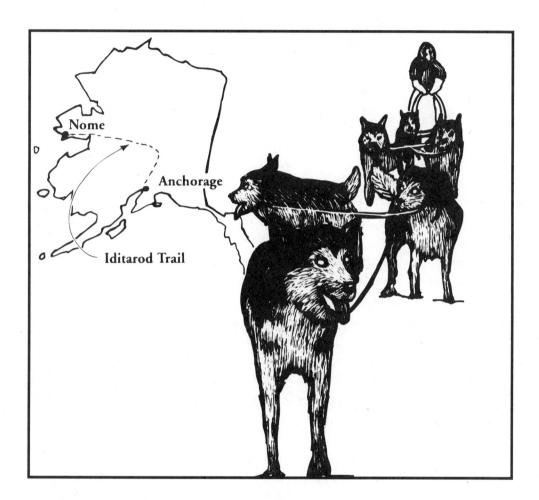

LESSON

5

Pre-reading Questions

1. What is the Iditarod?

2. Who runs in the race?

3. How is the weather during the race?

The Iditarod

Every year in early March, dogs pull sleds in a **race** along the Iditarod Trail. This **trail** is 1,770 kilometers long. It goes from Anchorage to Nome, Alaska. The people who drive the
5 dog **teams** are called **mushers.**

place to walk

A musher is an **adventurer.** He runs **by himself** with his dogs. Some mushers are women. Susan Butcher is a famous musher. She won the Iditarod race four times. Rick Swenson
10 won the race five times.

alone

Mushers are very **brave** to go on this adventure. The dogs run across snow and ice pulling their sleds. Sometimes the mushers ride, and sometimes they walk. In 1991, Rick
15 Swenson led his dogs through a snow storm. It was so dark that no one could see. He fell to his **knees** and got up again. In 1990, Susan Butcher's dogs got sick. Then they came to a river where there was water on top of ice.
20 They were very **lucky** that they didn't fall through the thin ice. No one could live in the icy water below.

knee

At night the mushers sleep in tents. In the morning they can see **footprints** of wild
25 animals near the camp. Sometimes they have to **shoot** at the wild animals to make them go away.

footprints

shoot

30   The Iditarod race is very long, dangerous, and cold. The mushers spend eleven or twelve days running this race. The temperature can go down to –46 degrees C (minus forty-six degrees Celsius). The dogs and the mushers take care of each other during this adventure.

A Vocabulary

by himself	race	lucky	brave
adventure	adventurer	footprints	teams
mushers	trail	knees	shoot

1. A musher is an _____ .
2. Sometimes they have to _____ at the wild animals to make them go away.
3. Mushers are very _____ to go on this adventure.
4. In the morning they can see _____ of wild animals near the camp.
5. He fell to his _____ and got up again.
6. He runs _____ with his dogs.
7. They were very _____ that they didn't fall through the thin ice.
8. The people who drive the dog _____ are called
   _____ .
9. This _____ is 1,770 kilometers long.

B　Vocabulary (new context)

tent	footprints	brave	by myself
lucky	adventurer	trail	knees
race	adventure	shoots	team

1. Our volleyball _____ won the game.
2. I don't need your help. I can do it _____.
3. Junko Tabei had a great _____ when she climbed Mount Everest.
4. Lois lost her new gold pen, but then she found it in her car. She was very _____.
5. When a hunter finds an animal, he usually _____ it.
6. Your _____ are in the middle of your legs.
7. When you walk on the beach, you leave your _____ in the sand.
8. Junko Tabei is a _____ woman.
9. If he can win the _____, he will be famous.

C　Vocabulary Review

pickup	competition	map	shells
history	canoe	current	silver
gold	ambassador	jewelry	used to
club	chose	able	future

1. The teacher _____ someone to answer the next question.
2. Carol has some beautiful _____. Some of it is _____ and some is _____.
3. Did you have to study the _____ of North America?
4. The new _____ from France met with Queen Elizabeth.
5. Most Europeans can't get _____ Arabic music. It sounds strange to them.
6. Can you find Sarawak, India, and Burma on the _____? Are you _____ to find them?
7. Paul belongs to a photography _____ because he likes to take pictures.
8. It is fun to ride in a _____ on a river.
9. A _____ truck is very useful for a carpenter.
10. The Peru _____ brings cold water from Antarctica along the west coast of South America.

D Questions

1. In what month is the Iditarod race?
2. What is the weather like then in Alaska?
*3. Did Rick Swenson always ride in his sled?
4. How many other people travel with the mushers?
5. Why do mushers sometimes shoot at wild animals?
6. How do the mushers know that wild animals come near the camp at night?
*7. Why couldn't Susan Butcher's dogs see the ice?
8. Who won the race more times?
*9. How do the dogs and the mushers take care of each other?
*10. About how far each day do the dogs have to run?

E Comprehension: True/False/No Information

_____ 1. The end of the Iditarod race is in Anchorage, Alaska.
_____ 2. Susan Butcher is a young woman.
_____ 3. The first dog is called the musher.
_____ 4. Rick Swenson helped his dogs through a snow storm.
_____ 5. Susan Butcher's dogs didn't fall through the ice.
_____ 6. Sometimes wild animals come near the camps at night.
_____ 7. Rick Swenson went to the University of Anchorage.
_____ 8. The dogs eat a lot of food during the race.
_____ 9. The temperatures during the Iditarod are below freezing.
_____ 10. The mushers have radios to call for help.
_____ 11. Susan Butcher's team won more races than Rick Swenson's team.

F Main Idea

1. Susan Butcher won the Iditarod four times.
2. Mushers and their dogs take care of each other.
3. The Iditarod is a big adventure.

Word Study

A Past Continuous

The past continuous is like the present continuous, but it shows something that continued to happen in the past. Use **was/were** instead of **am/is/are** and the **-ing** form of the verb.

> Example: It is 5:00. Glen **is studying.**
> At 5:00 yesterday, Glen **was studying.**

We often use the past continuous to show that one action interrupted another action. Use the simple past for the other verb.

> Example: Glen **was studying** when the phone **rang.**
> The phone **rang** while Glen **was studying.**

We usually use the past after **when** and the past continuous after **while.** (**when** + past, **while** + past continuous)

Put the correct form of the verb in the blank.

1. While Mr. Brooke (travel) _____ in Asia, there (be) _____ problems in Sarawak.
2. While David (walk) _____, he (fall) _____ through the ice.
3. A bear (try) _____ to pull him out of his tent while he (sleep) _____.
4. Howard (injure) _____ his knee while he (play) _____ soccer.
5. At 7:00 yesterday, David (shave) _____.
6. Tony (ski) _____ when it (start) _____ to snow.
7. Ann (enter) _____ the building when she (see) _____ an old friend.
8. Jean (sleep) _____ when the doorbell (ring) _____.
9. Ali (leave) _____ the classroom when the teacher (speak) _____ to him.
10. While Marie (write) _____ a letter, Pierre (telephone) _____ her.

B Spelling Review

1. Add **-y** to these nouns. Make an adjective.

   noise   storm   rock   wave

2. Add **-ing** to these verbs.

   study   plan   write   go

   swim   fly   bring   come

3. Write the plural form of these nouns.

   century   sandwich   knife   child

   adventure   gift   governor   day

4. Write the past tense of these verbs.

   try   mix   invent   belong

   defeat   shop   carry   play

5. Add **-est** to these adjectives.

   big   thick   heavy   low

   high   safe   small   hot

C Word Forms

	Verb	Noun	Adjective
1.		danger	dangerous
2.	invent	invention	
		inventor	
3.		science	scientific
		scientist	
4.	explore	exploration	
		explorer	
5.	sail	sail	
		sailor	
6.	be born	birth	
7.	lead	leader	
8.	rule	ruler	
9.	organize	organization	
10.	injure	injury	

Put the right word form in the blanks. Choose a word from Line 1 for Sentence 1, and so on. Use the right tenses. Some nouns are plural.

1. Always think about the ―――――――― when you walk across the street.
2. The computer is a wonderful ――――――――.
3. Kumiko plans to study ―――――――― and be a ――――――――.
4. Captain Cook ―――――――― the Pacific Ocean in the eighteenth century. He was an ――――――――.
5. ―――――――― did the work on sailing ships. These ships had ―――――――― to catch the wind. They ―――――――― all over the world.
6. The ―――――――― of a child makes the family very happy.
7. The captain will ―――――――― the soldiers into the town.
8. A king ―――――――― his country. He might be a good ―――――――― and he might not be.
9. You need to ―――――――― your compositions better. Good ―――――――― is important in compositions.
10. Oscar's car hit a tree. He has several ――――――――.

D Irregular Verbs

1. Learn these verb forms. Then use the past of each verb in a sentence.

	Simple	**Past**		**Simple**	**Past**
a.	choose	chose	e.	fall	fell
b.	leave	left	f.	meet	met
c.	spend	spent	g.	sleep	slept
d.	send	sent	h.	understand	understood

2. Write the past tense of these verbs.

a.	be ――――――――	g.	begin ――――――――
b.	blow ――――――――	h.	cut ――――――――
c.	do ――――――――	i.	find ――――――――
d.	get ――――――――	j.	give ――――――――
e.	know ――――――――	k.	put ――――――――
f.	ring ――――――――	l.	sell ――――――――

E Writing

Write real information in your answers.

1. Which lesson in *Unit 7* was the most interesting for you? Why?
2. You can travel through time and go with the people on one of the adventures in *Unit 7*. Which adventure will you go on? Why?
3. Describe an adventure of an important explorer in your country.

Video Highlights

A Before You Watch

You have read about the Iditarod. Now answer these questions.

1. What is the Iditarod?

   _____

2. Who are mushers?

   _____

3. Do you think that the Iditarod is a dangerous adventure? Why or why not?

   _____

B As You Watch

©CNN

Finish this sentence with at least two more reasons.

The dogs are important to the mushers because . . .
> . . . *the dogs are like pets for them.*

1. _____

2. _____

C After You Watch

1. *Think about the Iditarod*
   In the video, you heard two points of view. On one side, there are the **animal activists.** They are worried about the dogs and they want the race to stop. On the other side there are the **mushers.** They say that the race should continue.

2. *Take a Side*
   Which side are you on? Do you agree with the animal activists or the mushers? Add two more reasons under the side you choose.

Animal Activists   **Mushers**

Example: *The dogs are tied up when*   Example: *The race is a tradition in*
they are not racing.   *Alaska.*

1. _____   1. _____

   _____   _____

2. _____   2. _____

   _____   _____

3. Read your reasons aloud to the class. How many people in the class think the race should continue? How many think it should end?

Activity Page

A Go On an Adventure

Pretend you are a famous explorer. Think of what you will need to take with you. Use the pictures to help you think of the words.

Example: To sleep at night, I will need a *tent*.

1. To travel long distances across the sea like the Polynesians, I am going to need a _____.

2. To travel across the desert, I must have a _____ to ride on.

3. To travel across the snow in Alaska, I will need a _____ to pull my sled.

4. To hike over tall mountains where the snow is deep, I will need _____.

5. To dive with the dolphins in Honduras, I will need a suit made of _____.

B Travel Plans

Work with a partner. Decide where you would both like to go. Together, write a sentence explaining what you want to do when you get there. Then make a list of the things you will need to bring with you. Tell about your trip and read your list to the class.

We're going to visit Alaska to see the Iditarod. We'll need heavy coats, boots, gloves, sunglasses…

Dictionary Page

Finding Synonyms

Synonyms are words that have the same (or very similar) meanings. Not all words have synonyms.

1. Read the first definition of the word *gift*. What is its synonym?

> **gift** /gɪft/ *noun*
> **1** something given freely to another, *(synonym)* a present: *My father gave me a watch as a birthday gift.*
> **2** a special natural ability: *She has a gift for languages; she can speak five different languages.*

2. Draw lines between the following words and their synonyms. Use your dictionary to check your work.

defeat	happy
gift	decide
lucky	free
choose	fortunate
independent	present
terrible	horrible
glad	beat

3. Work with a partner. Partner A reads each sentence aloud. Partner B repeats the same sentence, but substitutes a synonym for the underlined word.

Example:
> Partner A: "Saudi Arabia <u>defeated</u> France in the soccer match."
> Partner B: "Saudi Arabia beat France in the soccer match."

a. The Polynesians were <u>lucky</u> to find such a beautiful island.
b. Tamerlane was probably very <u>glad</u> to have such an unusual present.
c. We don't know why Junko Tebei <u>chose</u> to climb the highest mountain in the world.

Vocabulary

A

able   233
about   7
above   17
across   189
add   114
adult   151
adventurer   244
afraid   12
age   195
ago   73
agree   207
alarm   162
alive   17
all over   7
alone   124
already   53
also   7
ambassador   228
among   207
appear   161
application   151
aquarium   22
area   161
army   109
around   88
arrive   207
art   73
at all   156
attend   190
avalanche   233
axe   195

B

bake   130
bamboo   195
band   119
basket   73
be able   233
beak   3
bear   12
beard   189
beat   129
become   78
believe   22
bell   167
belong to   239
below   151
beside   17
better   78

blow   201
blues   114
boring   119
both   58
bottle   125
brave   244
breathe   17
broom   84
burn   73
button   37
by himself   244

C

caffeine   124
calm   124
camel   7
can   125
canoe   223
card   129
carry   37
catch   12
cattle   124
century   114
cheap   47
chimney   167
chose   233
classical   109
climb   37
cloth   196
cloud   42
club   233
coast   183
collect   47
colony   207
comfortable   184
common   129
compact disc   119
company   119
competition   208
completely   189
composer   109
computer   156
continue   190
cool   7
could   37
country   124
cover   146
crop   78
current   223

D

dance   58
dangerous   124
dark   151
date   73
dead   201
death   240
deep   183
defeat   239
describe   7
desert   7
design   109
difficult   58
dig   146
dirt   146
disease   78
dolphin   22
double   223
during   3

E

each other   58
earn   93
earth   42
eastern   83
efficient   156
either   124
electronic   156
elevator   37
emotion   109
enemy   47
energy   78
engineer   146
enjoy   53
enough   167
enter   167
environmental   146
equipment   167
evaporate   42
even   83
ever   201
expensive   47
explorer   223
express   114
eyelash   7

F

factory   146
famous   42
fan   119

257

Skills Index

Irregular Verbs

Simple	Past	Simple	Past
be	was, were	hear	heard
become	became	hit	hit
begin	began	hurt	hurt
blow	blew	keep	kept
bring	brought	know	knew
build	built	lead	led
buy	bought	leave	left
catch	caught	lose	lost
choose	chose	make	made
come	came	meet	met
cut	cut	pay	paid
do (does)	did	put	put
drink	drank	ring	rang
drive	drove	run	ran
eat	ate	see	saw
fall	fell	sell	sold
feel	felt	send	sent
fight	fought	sleep	slept
find	found	slide	slid
fly	flew	speak	spoke
forget	forgot	spend	spent
freeze	froze	sweep	swept
get	got	take	took
give	gave	teach	taught
go (goes)	went	tell	told
grow	grew	think	thought
have (has)	had	understand	understood
		wear	wore
		win	won
		write	wrote

ARCTIC OCEAN

GREENLAND

Alaska (U.S.)

Baffin Bay

Yukon Territory

Northwest Territories

British Columbia

Alberta

Hudson Bay

C A N A D A Manitoba

Saskatchewan

Newfoundland

Quebec

Washington

Prince Edward Island

Ontario

New Hampshire

New Brunswick

Montana

North Dakota Minnesota

Vermont

Maine

Oregon

Idaho

Wisconsin

Nova Scotia

Wyoming

South Dakota

Michigan

New York

Massachusetts

Nevada

Utah

Nebraska

Iowa

Rhode Island
Connecticut

U N I T E D   S T A T E S

Illinois

Indiana

Ohio

Pennsylvania

New Jersey
Maryland
Delaware

California

Colorado

Kansas

West Virginia

Virginia

Washington D.C.

Missouri

Kentucky

Arizona

New Mexico

Oklahoma

Arkansas

Tennessee

North Carolina

South Carolina

PACIFIC OCEAN

Texas

Mississippi

Alabama Georgia

ATLANTIC OCEAN

Louisiana

M E X I C O

Hawaii

Gulf of Mexico

Florida

PUERTO RICO

NORTH

WEST   EAST

SOUTH

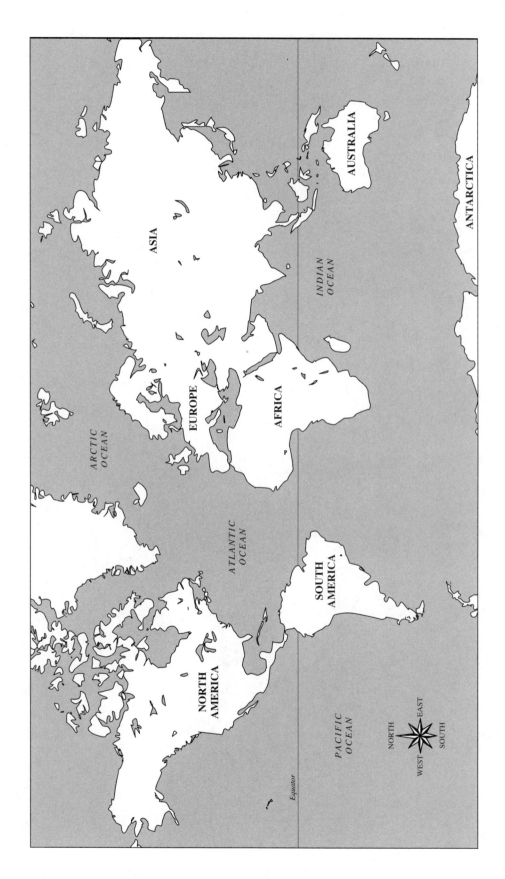

267